/4-1

WITNESS

By the same Author

Learning to Love God
Learning to Love Ourselves
Learning to Love People

WITNESS

A manual for use by small groups of
Christians who are serious in their desire
to learn how to share their faith.

Richard Peace

Foreword by Bruce Larson

ZONDERVAN PUBLISHING HOUSE
Grand Rapids, Michigan

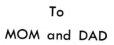

To
MOM and DAD

CONTENTS

Foreword — *Bruce Larson*

Introduction

Acknowledgments

One of the remarkable things about our day, in terms of leadership in the church as well as in the secular world, is that there is no adequate "school of the prophets" where one can go to be trained and equipped for leadership. The reason for this is simple. God is doing a new thing in this time of Reformation or Renaissance or Emergence. Therefore, God's "leaders" are being raised up through all kinds of unconventional means.

Richard Peace is one such leader. For the past several years, his "school" has been the Republic of South Africa.

There are four things about Richard Peace and his book that combine to make a unique package.

First, he is a statesman — a statesman for Jesus Christ and His Kingdom. The Kingdom of our Lord has always needed statesmen who can think beyond traditional boundaries and begin to see interlocking systems, denominations, cultures and subcultures.

Second, he is an evangelist. He sees that at the heart of the church in any age is the need for evangelists who can introduce others to Jesus Christ. But beyond that, Richard Peace is an equipper and enabler of evangelists.

His third remarkable trait or gift is that he is a strategist. Not only has he seen the need to train and equip laymen to be evangelists, but he has seen how this could be done. This gift of strategy is a fantastic gift.

Finally, he is an entrepreneur for the Holy Spirit. An entrepreneur is a rare breed — in business or in the spiritual realm. He senses when a market is ready for a new product, and puts together teams to produce the product and supply the needs of the market. Richard Peace has collected creative resources from all across the world and put them together into a package for which laymen everywhere are ready and eager.

This book is the result. It is an exciting book. Few people are as much in touch with creative forces as is Richard

Peace. He has put together something that has been of real value to laymen in South Africa and that now will be tremendously useful to laymen in the United States and other countries.

With a great deal of appreciation for Richard Peace and what his book represents, I commend this volume as an exciting training and equipping manual for the lay apostolate in the emerging church today.

BRUCE LARSON
Executive Director, *Faith at Work*

In recent years the Church has re-discovered an old truth: namely that the work of ministry is meant to be done *by the layman*. It has also become evident that part of this work of ministry involves evangelism. It is the layman's job to spread the Good News about Jesus.

But of course he cannot do this on his own without any training. And this is where *Witness* comes in. The intention of the course outlined in this book is to train laymen in the ministry of witness and evangelism.

This course has developed out of eight years of attempting to train laymen in this way. At first I conceived of lay-training solely in terms of "counselor-training," i.e. training lay people to help inquirers at evangelistic meetings. But it quickly became evident that this type of training was too specific and of too little use outside the context of mass evangelism. Surely one could train laymen in such a way that they could, on their own, evangelize without having to wait for an evangelist to come to town. In fact, was this not what St. Paul urged those called to evangelism to do first and foremost? "Christ gave to the Church some men to be . . . Evangelists . . . for the purpose of equipping God's people so that they (God's people) could do the work of ministry" — part of which is evangelism (Ephesians 4:11, 12, Free translation).

There are two foci to this training course. The first intention is to help the layman learn how to share his faith on an individual basis. This is the usual subject of books like this. The second intention is to help the layman learn how to share his faith *alongside his brothers in Christ by means of small groups*. This is, perhaps, the unique feature of *Witness*.

It seems to me that for too long a time we have understood witness in too individualistic a sense. The idea has been that the norm is for the individual layman to be out alone in the world bearing witness. We have lost the idea of witness *as a community*. Yet it seems to be self-evident that a small band of fellowshiping Christians, evangelizing together, would be far more effective than the sum of the witness of each individual on his own. Not that individual witness would cease. Rather the individual would receive his strength and motivation from the fellowship — becoming a more effective individual witness. And then, added to this, would be the witness of the body together by means of small groups.

In 1970 these ideas were put to test in Johannesburg, South Africa, where this course was used during a city-wide interdenominational preaching mission. Nearly 500 training groups were established. Most of these developed into outreach groups. Not only did Christian laymen seem to benefit from the training, and actually start to evangelize on their own, but non-Christians were attracted to the outreach groups and many discovered the reality of Jesus through these.

Although this book is intended to be used as a guide for a group, it can be read with profit (I trust) by an individual on his own. However, if the individual can recruit six or so of his friends and together start a group, the book will be far more meaningful. Then *Witness* will not become just another theoretical guide, but will serve as a blueprint for action.

Nature of the Program

As I have indicated, this course has been arranged to take place in small groups. There are several reasons for this from a learning point of view. For one thing, it has become clear in recent years that the most effective and long-lasting training occurs by means of small groups. I think the church is now beginning to learn this lesson. For far too long we have felt that the way to train people is to lecture them. We have thought that if people are presented with *correct ideas,* their attitudes and actions will change automatically. Unfortunately, this does not happen quite that easily. For an idea to change our attitudes and actions, we must not only accept the idea, we must also consciously *apply* the idea to ourselves and then deliberately *act* upon it. In a small group, unlike a lecture, we have the opportunity to discuss ideas and hence see how they apply to us and what action we must take.

Small groups are also valuable because of the support and encouragement they provide as we struggle along to become witnesses. Learning to be a witness is a frightening thing to many Christians. But in a group of like-minded friends it becomes possible to overcome our fears as the whole group learns together, shares together, encourages one another, and hence provides all the support needed. This cannot take place in the anonymity of a large lecture.

The Operation of the Group

A few words are in order about how the groups are meant to operate during the eight sessions. (Detailed outlines for each session are given in the Group Leader's Guide which accompanies this book. It is essential that the leader of the group possess this.)

Typically, a group will begin with some sort of brief (e.g. 15 minute) exercise (discussion; Bible study; writing, etc.) designed to prepare the group for the lecture that follows.

Next, a brief recorded lecture will be played* — or given in summary form by the group leader. (These lectures are printed in an expanded version in this book.) Each lecture is designed to present certain essential data about witnessing and outreach. During the lecture you will be asked to take notes, which will not only aid you in concentrating on the lecture, but will also serve as the basis for the ensuing discussion.

Following this there will be a longer (e.g. 30 minute) group exercise. The aim of each of the exercises will be to try to come to grips in a practical way with the ideas that have been presented. The exercises for each session are outlined in this Manual.

---

*available on a cassette from Zondervan Publishing House.

The Use of the Manual

This Manual is designed to assist you in private study during the week which follows each group session. If you glance through it you will see that your "homework" each week will consist of:

1. *Reading*

The first thing you ought to do each week is to read over the text of the *lecture,* which was given during the group session, to make sure you have *understood* what was presented. However, what you read will not be a mere repeat of what you heard. It will, in fact, be an amplification and further development of the key ideas.

If by some chance you miss one of the group sessions (and it is hoped that only absolutely major problems — e.g. your house is burning down! — will keep you away) you can catch up by reading the lecture, though of course you will miss the exercises, and will be missed by the group.

From the lecture, move on in your reading to the supplementary material found in some of the chapters. These brief statements, drawn from a variety of sources, will serve to highlight certain main ideas.

Finally, in the bibliography are listed those particular books which deal with the key subjects under discussion in each chapter should you wish to pursue your study further (now, or later on).

2. *Study*

Once your reading is complete, move on to the study exercises. Each of these exercises aims at helping you to *apply to yourself* the ideas which you have read about. The exercises are often "mirrors," in that you will see yourself in the light of the presentation in the chapter — and hence be able to say, "Yes, now this is how the ideas apply to my life." Incidentally, you may want to keep your work private at this stage, in that many of these exercises are intended to help you express your real thoughts and feelings (and not just to put down the "correct" answers). Some people will not feel free to do this if they know others will be looking over their shoulder, reading what they write. However, I hope that they will ultimately want to share what they discover with others, particularly those in their group. These exercises are not intended to be graded by anyone.

3. Action

The "action" section is the next logical step in the application of the ideas. You are asked actually to *do* something. This is really what the course is all about — learning to *be* a witness, not just learning *about* witnessing.

What you are asked to do, however, is never difficult. You are asked, in some small way, to start putting into practice the ideas you have studied. You will not be alone in this. Your whole group will be doing the same thing — and then sharing the results at next week's session.

Method of Study

Several comments are in order if you are to get the most out of your individual study. For one thing, you must try to find a *quiet place* in which to work. To work in the living room while the rest of the family is there watching television is hopeless. Pick a place where you will not be disturbed. This may even mean sitting in the car in the garage, as one friend I know did in order to study the Bible!

Furthermore, set aside a *regular time* to study, if at all possible. You do not need long. You can get through the homework if you spend 15 minutes a day. Incidentally, it is far better to do a little each day, than to try and do it all at once, two hours before the group session! Time will be available if you set your mind to finding it.

The patterns of study you develop over this 8 week period may become far more significant than you realize. They may develop into fixed patterns of Bible study and prayer — one of the keys to developing a deep relationship with our Lord.

An Overall Plan

Having discussed this training course itself, it will be useful to put it in the context of a total evangelistic program. The scheme which is outlined on the following chart is one which has been used profitably by individual groups, by churches, and in at least one instance, by nearly 200 churches which had banded together for a city-wide preaching mission.

On the chart you will notice that the training group as outlined in *Witness* provides the foundation for the whole endeavor. Following the eight training sessions (plus the one Outreach Evening which is part of the course), the group splits into two or three smaller outreach groups. Each sub-group becomes an action-unit, with the aim of doing evangelism by means of small groups — for three to six weeks.

Following this, a series of evangelistic meetings could be held, at which an individual (or individuals) would seek to articulate via lectures the nature of the Christian Gospel, giving an opportunity then and there for a personal response to Christ's call to follow Him. These meetings would serve to consolidate for those non-Christians attending the outreach groups the discussion which had taken place in previous weeks.

Finally, the whole endeavor could be rounded-off by a series of four to seven weeks of Bible study in which the question considered would be: What does it mean to live in this world as a Christian?

This is the ideal plan. Of course, not every group will be able to follow it exactly. But it is important to remember that the aim of the whole course is to train Christians to do outreach by means of small groups, as well as on an individual level. And for this training to be meaningful it must be used.

Personal Responsibility

For you to benefit from this course will require a certain amount of sacrifice on your part. It is important that this be clear right at the beginning. Schedules will have to be altered temporarily to make way for group meetings. Time is also going to have to be snatched from your already busy day to be used in reading and study. Even more difficult, perhaps, you are going to have to open yourself up to new ideas and new patterns of relationships. This is never easy. Yet all of this is part of what is involved in following Christ. He really is in the process of remaking us into the sort of people He always wanted us to be. And this requires from us our time, our sacrifice, and our openness. Yet, in the end, it is all for the best. As our faith in Christ comes alive in new ways, so too we come alive as people.

As I write about commitment in this course, I cannot help but recall the words of Douglas Hyde, an ex-Communist, now a Christian, who once commented on the secret of the success of the Communist movement.

> What distinguishes the Communist movement from most others and makes it possible for so small a minority to make so great an impact upon our time is the dedication of the average individual member and the immense and dynamic force this represents when all those individuals collectively make their contribution to the cause. Without that they would not be prepared to accept the organization, the discipline, the unending "Marxist education," the incessant appeals for even more action . . . There is no mystery about the indisputable fact that Communists exert an influence out of all proportion to their numbers, once one grasps the point that practically every party member is a dedicated man in whose life, from the time he rises in the morning till the time he goes to bed at night, for 365 days of the year, Communism is the dominant force.[1]

May God give each of us the grace to take as seriously our task of sharing the Good News of Christ as the Com-

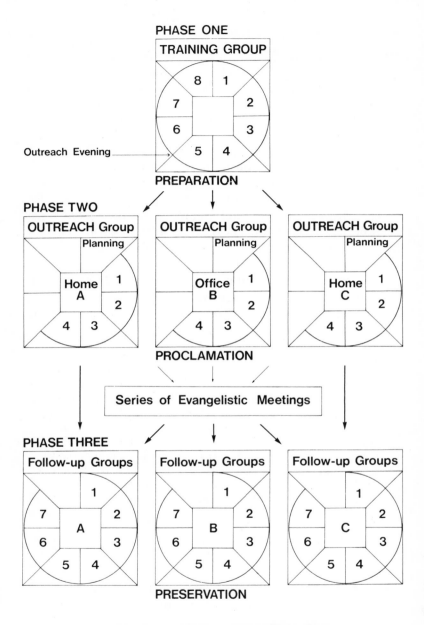

A PLAN FOR EVANGELISM

munists take the spreading of their economic and political theories.

> *O Lord, grant that I will be given*
> *eyes to see the needs of those around me;*
> *a heart to be concerned over what I see;*
> *and the will to do all I can to share*
> *the Gospel in the face of this.*
> *Forgive me for my past hesitation*
> *and lack of concern.*
> *Arm me with new dedication,*
> *new zeal, new ability and most of all,*
> *with a new sense of Your power and*
> *presence in my life.*
>
> *Amen.*

Acknowledgments

A book of this nature cannot really be written just by sitting down and thinking: "Now what ought to go into a good training course?" Rather, it develops slowly over a long period of time out of the experience of actually trying to train laymen. Consequently, this book has been influenced by many individuals. I only wish it were possible to remember and thus acknowledge all such by name.

In particular I am grateful for the opportunity afforded me by African Enterprise to conduct training courses in Ladysmith, Cape Town, Nairobi, and Johannesburg as part of missions conducted in these cities. I value greatly the interaction with the material on the part of various individuals taking these courses.

I am indebted as well to those who in a special way helped to produce this book: to Dr. Donald Ehat who first stimulated me to think about the nature of adult training and provided many valuable clues as to how it could best be done; to Bishop John Carter, Michael Cassidy, Christian Smith and Antony Taylor whose perceptive reading of the manual gave me new insights into it; and to Rebecca Tsekeletsa, Wendy Reid, John Tooke and Alethea Candiotes, all of whom aided in the myriad details of production.

A special word of thanks to Peter Eliastam for the suggested design and layout of the book; to Jennifer Aitchison for the artwork; to Veronica Engelbrecht who gave invaluable and sustained help in translating the manuscript from written scrawl into a proper book; to Loraine Evans who not only typed this manuscript twice, but interacted perceptively with the ideas; to Jack Cook for the stimulation of his many ideas born out of his vast experience in training lay people, for his detailed and penetrating examination of the manual, as well as for his experimentation with the course in test groups; and to my wife Judy, who not only gave up many evenings and weekends while I was writing the book, but also was the source of many of the key ideas.

Grateful acknowledgment is made to the following publishers for permission to reprint copyrighted material:

GEOFFREY BLES, LTD. for excerpts from C. S. Lewis, *Mere Christianity*, © 1962; *Christian Reflections*, © 1967; *A Mind Awake* (edited by Clyde S. Kilby), © 1968 by the executors of the estate of C. S. Lewis; and J. B. Phillips, *The New Testament in Modern English*, © 1958 by J. B. Phillips.

REV. A.J.T. COOK for excerpts from *Handbook of Lay Involvement*.

THE DIVISION OF CHRISTIAN EDUCATION OF THE NATIONAL COUNCIL OF THE CHURCHES OF CHRIST for quotations from the Revised Standard Version of the Bible, © 1946 and 1952.

WM. B. EERDMANS PUBLISHING COMPANY for excerpts from C. S. Lewis, *Christian Reflections*, © 1967 by the executors of the estate of C. S. Lewis; Mary McDermott Shideler, *A Creed for a Christian Skeptic*, © 1968; and John Stott, *Basic Christianity*, © 1958.

THE BILLY GRAHAM EVANGELISTIC ASSOCIATION for excerpts from Leighton Ford, *Letters to a New Christian*, © 1967 by Leighton Ford.

GUIDEPOSTS MAGAZINE for excerpts from *Get Going Through Small Groups* by George and Florence Pert, © 1969 by Guideposts Associates, Inc.

THE HALFWAY HOUSE for excerpts from "A New Breed of Men" by Bruce Larson found in *Groups in Action*, © 1968 by Lyman Coleman.

HARCOURT, BRACE, JOVANOVICH, INC. for excerpts from C. S. Lewis, *A Mind Awake* (edited by Clyde S. Kilby), © 1969 by the executors of the estate of C. S. Lewis.

HARPER AND ROW PUBLISHERS, INC. for excerpts from Dietrich Bonhoeffer, *Life Together*, © 1954; Leighton Ford, *The Christian Persuader*, © 1966 by Leighton Ford; D. T. Niles, *That They May Have Life*, © 1951; Clyde Reid, *Groups Alive — Church Alive*, © 1969 by Clyde Reid; and Samuel Shoemaker, *The Experiment of Faith*, © 1957 by Samuel Shoemaker.

HERALD PRESS for excerpts from Paul Miller, *Group Dynamics in Evangelism*, © 1958.

Chapter 1

The Principles of Witness

The Principles of Witness

Group Exercises

PHASE I: *Getting to Know One Another* (30 minutes)

The first order of business is to get to know the people in your group since they will be sharing with you in this whole training experience.

To facilitate this, each person in the circle will be asked to answer three questions as a means of introducing himself. You have three minutes to collect your thoughts. There is room to make brief notes below each question as you do so.

1. FACTS ABOUT YOURSELF:

Give your name. Where were you born? Tell the group about your family (if you are married). When did you move to this area? (Take only thirty seconds when sharing this with the group, so that everyone will have a chance to speak).

2. FACTS ABOUT YOUR INTERESTS:

Start by giving your name again (people may have missed it the first time). What really excites you? What do you most enjoy? Is it gardening? (tell the group about this hobby). Or is it sports? Or reading? Or your job? (Take one minute to share this).

3. FACTS ABOUT YOUR EXPERIENCE OF GOD:

This is a voluntary question. We will not go around the circle this time, but the leader will ask whoever wishes to answer the question: "When, if ever, did 'God' become more than a word to you?"

Even though it is optional, do try to share at this point. It will help the group to know a bit about the real "you" as well as giving you the chance to try to put into words your own experience of God. Begin, once again, by giving your name.

PHASE II: *The Lecture* (15 minutes)

Sit back now and listen to the first lecture. To help you to concentrate and to prepare for Phase III, answer the questions which follow *while the tape is playing*. You need only make brief notes. The lecture deals with each question in order. Incidentally, no one will be "examining" your answers to see if they are right! They will, however, serve as the basis for the discussion which will follow the lecture. Read all the questions first, before the tape starts.

1. Why do we do evangelism?

2. What is the key principle of evangelism?

3. What does common sense tell us about the validity of the Biblical principle of evangelism?

4. What does mathematics tell us?

5. What does history tell us?

PHASE III: *Evangelism and Me* (45 minutes)

The leader will now introduce a discussion centering on how these principles can actually be applied.

Study Schedule

READ:

1. *The Foreword and Introduction,* to understand how the training course operates.

2. *The Text of the Lecture,* asking yourself, "What is Christ's plan for the Church and where do I fit into it?"

3. *The Supplementary Paper,* "The Spontaneous Missionary Church," asking yourself, "How does the first century church compare with the modern church, and what can we learn from those early days?"

4. *Sections from those books in the Bibliography* which deal with aspects of this lecture which especially puzzle or interest you.

CONSIDER FOR YOURSELF:

"Ephesians 4 and Me," so as to apply this key concept of evangelism to your life.

ACT:

1. *By contacting Christian friends* from your area to invite them to join your training group, striving to bring into the group at least one new person.

2. *By delivering the Training Manual* as soon as possible to those who have agreed to come, so they can catch up with what they missed in the first session. (No one will be able to join your group after the next meeting.)

The Principles of Evangelism

"A church which bottlenecks its outreach by depending on its specialists — its pastors or evangelists — to do its witnessing, is living in violation of both the intention of its Head and the consistent pattern of the early Christians."[1]

Leighton Ford

Evangelism begins when we start to take seriously the so-called "Great Commission" which our Lord gave to His Church: "You must go out to the whole world and proclaim the Gospel to every creature."[2] These are quite staggering words. "Go out to the *whole world.*" He did not say: "Go only to Jerusalem." "Preach . . . to *every creature.*" He did not say "Preach only to the Jews." The command was total. Our commission was to evangelize all the people on the earth.

This commission has never been rescinded. It is as valid today as it was in the first century. And as loyal disciples, tempting as it may be, we have no right to reduce the scope of our Lord's commission to fit our own vision; or to limit our evangelizing to suit our own inclinations.

THE BIBLICAL PRINCIPLE OF MINISTRY

I remember how baffled I was when I first realized what our Lord was saying in the Great Commission. "Preach to *every* creature." "Impossible," was my reaction — "a great idea, and useful as a guideline, but certainly not realizable." How *could* the Gospel be preached to everyone? Think what a task this would have been even in the first century when the commission was originally given. There were only a few disciples then and the Roman Empire was vast. How much more difficult the task is today with our more than three billion people. Did our Lord then give us an impossible commission?

The more I thought about this, the more I felt that this

30

could not be so. But yet, *how* could we preach to the world? How? This was the key question.

Then I came upon Ephesians 4:11-12 — and as I read this statement by St. Paul on the nature of the Church, it was as if a great light suddenly flashed on. I *saw* how we could, in fact, do what our Lord commanded us.

These verses read like this:

> And Christ gave to the Church some men to be Apostles, some to be Prophets, some to be Evangelists, some to be Pastors and Teachers, for the purpose of equipping God's people so they should do the work of the ministry with a view to the building up of the body of Christ.

What St. Paul is saying here is so self-evident when one thinks about it. (Why had I not seen it before?) The work of ministry (part of which is evangelism, or "preaching the Gospel") is meant to be done by all of "God's people," that is, by the layman, by the average man and woman who is a follower of Christ. Ministry is not the job of the minister! *Ministry is the job of the layman.* Ministry is your job and my job. The job of the minister, i.e. the full-time "professional" person (be he Pastor, Teacher, Evangelist, Prophet or Apostle) is to *train us to do our job of ministry!*

I suddenly realized that here was the key to world evangelization — every Christian everywhere sharing the Gospel. All along I had been baffled by the Great Commission because I had assumed that this "preaching the Gospel" could only really be done by the full-time Christian minister or evangelist. (Was this as a result of my experience of how churches in fact operate?) Of course there would never be enough evangelists or ministers to reach the whole world.

But there are enough lay people. Almost one third of the world is Christian (at least nominally).[3] We can, if we will, "preach the Gospel to every creature."

COMMON SENSE SUPPORTS THIS PRINCIPLE

Of course this makes real sense when you think about it. A local church with 600 *de facto* ministers is bound to make more of an impact than a church with only one minister, plus a passive congregation numbering 600. It is strange then that in the present day Church we seem to have developed a pattern whereby the layman employs a minister to do the whole job of ministry, while he himself sits back as a spectator — cheering the pastor on and occasionally assisting the pastor — but seldom ministering himself, much less allowing the pastor to train him.

Leighton Ford points out that part of the blame for this misunderstanding of the nature of ministry may have to rest on a misplaced comma!

Amazingly, a tiny mistranslation in our Bibles may have contributed to our misunderstanding. We have been operating on "the fallacy of the misplaced comma" in the fourth chapter of Ephesians! In this famous passage Paul is describing the various gifts and offices which the risen Christ has given to the Church. Most of the older versions and some newer ones translate Ephesians 4:11-12 in this sense: "And his gifts were that some should be apostles, some prophets, some evangelists, some pastors and teachers, for the equipment of the saints, for the work of the ministry, for building up the body of Christ."

The apparent meaning of this is that the evangelist (or pastor) has a threefold task: (1) to equip the saints; (2) to do the work of ministry; (3) to build up the Body of Christ. Actually, there should be *no comma* between these first two phrases. Even a different preposition is used. In "for the equipment of the saints" it is "pros," while in "for the work of the ministry" it is "eis" or, as it would be better to say, "*unto* the work of ministry." A more accurate translation, then, runs: "And these were his gifts: some to be apostles, some prophets, some evangelists, some pastors and teachers, *to equip God's people for work in his service* . . ." (NEB, italics mine). Or as Phillips correctly paraphrases, "His gifts were made *that Christians might be properly equipped for their service.*"

The error is a small one in grammar, but a great one in practical consequences. For it now appears that the clergy's main task is not to do the work of the church, but to equip God's people to do this work . . .

In terms of evangelism, the old pattern will not do. It is not enough for the layman to *pay* the preacher to win souls, or even help him to do so. The pattern is that *the minister helps the layman* to evangelize! . . .

To use Elton Trueblood's analogy, Christians are not like members of an orchestra society, who hire musicians and a conductor and sit back to enjoy the performance. They are members of the orchestra. Each has a part to play, and the minister is the conductor who helps each to fit in, as a whole orchestra presents a glorious symphony of praise to Christ.[4]

MATHEMATICS ILLUSTRATES THIS PRINCIPLE

Lest you remain skeptical of the possibility of preaching the Gospel to the whole world by acting on this Pauline principle, let me share some interesting mathematics. Assume for a moment that there is only one Christian on earth. Being a faithful Christian, however, he seeks to share the gospel message with others. And in six months' time his labors are rewarded. One of his friends becomes a Christian. Together now, these two Christians carry on sharing the Gospel. At the end of that first year, they each have won another to Christ. There are now four Christians.

This pattern continues through the second year. Each Christian wins one person to Christ every six months. The new converts in turn join the witnessing band. Hence in the middle of the second year, the four Christians have won four others, making a total of eight. These eight win eight others, making sixteen at the end of the second year. If this continues, at the end of the third year there will be sixty-four Christians. At the end of the fifth year there will be 1,024. Year by year the Christian community increases — more rapidly all the time. If this pattern continues unabated for just sixteen years there would be over four billion Christians — more than the present population of the whole earth! *Mathematically, in one generation, it is possible to preach the Gospel to every creature!*

Now of course it is clear to everyone that in the nearly 2,000 years we have had to preach the Gospel, by no one's count could the world be considered fully Christian. Why not? What went wrong? I think it is obvious. *All too few Christians are, in fact, sharing the Gospel with their friends.* Too many of us have opted out of our responsibility to be ministers for Christ's sake.[5]

HISTORY CONFIRMS THIS PRINCIPLE

It is not just by means of mathematics that we can verify the wisdom of St. Paul's principle that "every Christian is to be an evangelist." All we really need to do is to open a history of the church. It seems that down through the ages whenever this principle was put into practice, spectacular results followed.

Take, for example, the New Testament Church. The only way to account for the breathtaking spread of Christianity throughout the Mediterranean world is by noting the "ground-swell of spontaneous lay witness."[6] As has been pointed out, in the first century there were "no evangelizing campaigns, no mission boards and even little, if any, organized missionary activity. And yet, the Church was constantly growing."[7]

Origen, the early Church historian, tells us why. "Christians do all in their power to spread the faith over the world." Christians "went on, in every place . . . sowing the saving seed of the kingdom of heaven widely throughout the whole world." And *almost all of these itinerant preachers were laymen.*[8]

In the eighteenth century the great Wesleyan Revival shook England. While most people recognized that this movement was sparked off by John Wesley's preaching (aided by Charles Wesley's hymns) it is often forgotten that the movement grew, spread and was conserved as a direct result of the *small groups of laymen* which Wesley organized into witnessing bands.

In our time this principle has been vindicated in the experience of the church in South America. This church is now growing steadily as a direct result of training laymen to be active witnesses. This effort began not too many years ago. It grew out of the frustration experienced by one of the large missionary groups, the Latin America Mission.

In the mid-1950's, the Latin America Mission was worried. It had become evident to the leaders of the Mission that the Church was not coping very well with the job of evangelism. In fact, it was losing ground. The growth of the population far outstripped the growth of the Church. Hence each year, the percentage of the Christians within the population decreased!

When the Latin America Mission looked at the Church to see what could be done to improve matters, they were discouraged. The Church seemed to be suffering from a sort of deadness and paralysis. Tired, discouraged pastors preached trite sermons to listless congregations. The only time it seemed that interest could be roused was when yet another split in the Church was imminent over a minor point of doctrine.

Latin America Mission was discouraged with their own attempts to rectify matters. In the years after World War II they had greatly increased their staff of missionaries. In fact, they had doubled their numbers — and yet this seemed to have made no appreciable difference in terms of evangelism.

Maddening too was the fact that even though the Church was not growing, other movements — mostly non-Christian — were growing. Determined not to give up, the leaders of Latin America Mission decided instead to take a long, hard look at these rapidly growing movements to assess just what was their secret of success.

They looked at the Communist movement. In little over 100 years, starting from a small band of dedicated men, this anti-Christian movement had grown to control nearly one billion people world-wide. They looked as well at the Jehovah's Witnesses. This semi-Christian movement was growing at an annual rate of approximately 400 percent. They then looked at the one branch of the Christian Church in South America that was actually growing — the Pentecostals.

35

In only fifty years of work, this Christian movement had grown to fifteen million members.

What was the secret of success of these diverse movements? Certainly not a common message. What the Communist youth leader would say was almost directly opposite to the message of the Pentecostal pastor.

As Latin America Mission probed the nature of these movements the answer emerged. *What each had in common was the successful mobilization of their entire constituency in continuous outreach.* Latin America Mission put their findings together into a concise statement, the so-called Strachan theorem:[9] "The successful expansion of any movement is in direct proportion to its success in mobilising and occupying its total membership in constant propagation of its beliefs."[10]

I trust that by now this theorem sounds strangely familiar. It is really nothing more than a paraphase of Ephesians 4: 11-12. "Every layman is meant to be a full time evangelist!"

UNDERSTANDING THE BIBLICAL PRINCIPLE

I think it is clear by now that every Christian layman is called upon to be a witness for Christ. Now the question is: what does this mean? Are we expected to run out and corner the nearest person and say, "Listen, here is the Christian Gospel!"? This is the image many people conjure up when they hear the word "witness." Hence some definitions are in order.

Webster's Dictionary says that a witness is ". . . a person who . . . can give a first hand account of something." This is simple enough. Hence as Christian witnesses we are not called upon to make theological pronouncements about certain dogma, nor are we expected to give prophetic utterances about the state of modern society. We are simply called upon to "give an account of" the something (actually, the *someone*) of which we have a first hand knowledge. We are called upon to give a first hand account of Jesus Christ.

This we do in at least three distinct ways: through our involvement, through our life, and through our words.

1. Witness Through Involvement

We serve as witnesses when we involve ourselves in one way or another in evangelistic endeavors undertaken by the church. For example, some years ago I was involved in an outreach effort for youth. The churches in this particular community wanted to try to reach the real "outsiders" — i.e., those young people who never came near a church. They knew they could not do this by holding meetings in any church-owned buildings, so they decided to use homes as the venue for outreach. But running the project in this way meant that the help of a large number of lay people was needed. Group leaders were required. Hostesses were needed in the homes. Christian teenagers had to provide the music, etc. Now the question is: "Who were the witnesses in this project?" Only those few people who actually *spoke* at the home meetings? No, everyone who participated in the project, whether it was by writing out invitations or by speaking, was being a witness.

We must be clear at this point because sometimes witness in such a way is disparaged. "Oh, you are just typing mission letters because you are afraid to talk about Christ to others." This may be the case. But more than once have we seen a person lose his shyness and begin to be a witness in other more direct ways, as a result of his involvement in the seemingly mundane side of running a mission.

However, we must not ever be content just to type mission letters, or run the press to produce mission material. (This is not to deny the value of such activity. If a mission is to succeed, all these rather mechanical tasks must be performed.) Rather these activities ought to be only the first level of involvement in the whole work of witness. We must strive to couple to this, witness through our life and by our words.

2. Witness Through Our Life

We also witness through the sort of life we live. In this sense every one of us is a witness for Christ (either a good witness or a bad witness) because through our actions and attitudes we say a lot about Christianity to those around us. Here is a good example of this:

> I read recently of an American university student who tried to witness to her roommate but thought she had failed. The entire first term of her school year was a time of sickness and difficulty. To her amazement, when she came back after vacation she found that her roommate had become a Christian and gave as the reason, "I have watched the way you have suffered."[11]

The way we live is a form of witness. This is not to say we must pretend in a self-conscious way to be what we think a Christian ought to be, when in fact we are not that way. Such dishonesty puts others off — because it often comes through as smug piety. What does attract — and I will say more about this later — is a real person, facing real problems, in the awesome power of Christ.

What sort of life should we then strive for? What sort of life does witness? A good, perfect life? No, we are not told in Scripture to try to be good. We are told rather "to be devoted to Christ." There is a world of difference between the two. If we are devoted to Christ, goodness will follow naturally, whereas to make goodness, not Christ, our aim is to doom ourselves to failure and probably self-righteousness as well. St. Peter put it so well: "Simply concentrate on being completely devoted to Christ in your heart. Be ready at any time to give a quiet and reverent answer to any man who wants a reason for the hope that you have within you."[12]

3. Witness Through Words

This brings us to the third way in which we witness — through our words. Note that St. Peter says that if we live a life devoted to Christ, we will, quite naturally, be questioned about this. And when we are questioned, we ought to be able to express in words "the hope" that we have.

Leighton Ford's experience illustrates this beautifully:

> Last October we were in New Orleans. An attractive young couple asked my wife and me to lunch. As we drove along,

we discovered that they were leaders in the social and business life of that city and had only been Christians a year. Two years before, they had met a captivating couple from Oklahoma City. Immediately they noticed a difference in this couple. The newcomer to town was a successful businessman, but not a slave of the business "rat race." In his wife they had observed an absence of the catty little remarks about other women, and the malicious gossip to which they were so accustomed. Finally, after a year they could stand it no longer and they asked the new couple, "Why are you so different?" And they then heard the story of how those friends had found Christ in Oklahoma City at the Billy Graham Crusade. As a result this New Orleans couple committed their own lives to Christ.[13]

Ultimately, our aim is to be able to express in words the nature of our faith. We must learn to do so, clearly and accurately.

We are called to be witnesses for Christ— through our involvement, through our life, and through our words. *Our aim is to be involved in all three ways.* And as we do so, we become what we are called to be in this world — full-time evangelists for Christ's sake.

CONCLUSION

Let me summarize what I have been trying to say by putting all this in a slightly different way. Think for a moment about the world in which we live. It takes little reflection to see that it is a desperately needy place. If you doubt this — just pick up today's newspaper and circle in red all those items which deal with death, disease, international tensions, conflict or crime. You will soon find that your newspaper is a mass of red marks.

Even better, reflect for a moment upon your friends, associates, relatives or neighbors. What are their problems? What tensions are they facing? Are there marriage problems? Or teenagers whom parents just do not seem to understand? Is it illness? Trouble at work? The need of the world is not something "out there." It affects even those you know personally.

But you know what this thing of "need" is all about through your own experience. Turn your thoughts inward for a moment. As you do so make a mental check list of the problems you face, the tensions with which you live, the difficult relationships with which you have to cope.

It is obvious that the world is a sad place in many ways. There is difficulty without and within. The question is, how can we cope in the face of these problems? Must we simply resign ourselves to it all and plod along as best we can, hoping for the best?

"No" is the ringing answer Christianity gives to the question. Life is more, far more, than dull resignation. It is true that there are many problems. But *this is why Christ came.* He came into this difficult world in which we live and lived as a man and then died and rose again from the dead — and *is still alive today.* He is alive — and calling us into a relationship with Himself — a relationship of love and forgiveness, a relationship through which we are rescued from our inadequacies and made — slowly but surely — into the sort of people He originally created us to be. He did not come to take us out of the world, but to be with us in the world, giving us His love and power and so enabling us to cope — to be, as St. Paul put it "more than conquerors."

What an incredible message we have in the face of the needs of this world. *The world must hear this.* This is what it is waiting for.

But how will people hear this — "hear" in such a way as to grasp the significance of the message for themselves?

There is only one answer — the world must hear through us, the Christian laymen. And when we get on with the job and tell others this Good News, the world will begin to change. History has shown this. If we get on with our task our city will begin to change; our friends will change; we will grow and change.

But it is up to us. God has called us to proclaim this grand message. Dare we disobey?

Ephesians 4 and me

"And Christ gave to the Church some men to be Apostles, some to be Prophets, some to be Evangelists, some to be Pastors and Teachers, for the purpose of equipping God's people so that they should do the work of ministry with a view to the building up of the body of Christ."

St. Paul states here that the work of ministry (of which evangelism is a major part) is to be done by *every* member of Christ's Church. No one is excluded. All of "God's people" are included.

But how do you feel about this? Are you pleased to know this? Or depressed? In other words, what is your honest feeling about being called to take part in the ministry of evangelism?

Why do you feel this way?

What do you feel about the training course which has been launched as a direct attempt "to equip God's people so that they should do the work of ministry"? What are your hopes? What are your fears?

The Principles of Witness

"Having thought through my own feelings, I am willing to undertake this training course as an act of faith. Hence I commit myself before God to:

1. Give this course *top priority* for the next eight weeks, by attending faithfully, reading and studying diligently, and acting consistently to put into practice what I learn;

2. Open myself to the *influence of the Holy Spirit,* to learn from Him;

3. Open myself to the *power and presence of Christ* so as to come to know Him in a deeper, richer way;

4. Open myself to *my friends,* so as to share with them what I am learning of Christ;

5. Open myself to the *others in the group,* so as to learn from them and to share with them what I know from my own unique, God-given perspective."

If you are able freely to commit yourself in such a way, you will find your response of faith answered in ways you cannot begin to anticipate. May God give you the faith to do so.

Action

"Every Christian is to be a witness." One way in which to put this principle into action is by recruiting others to join your group. The more Christians involved, the wider the influence of Christ can be spread. So . . .

1. *Contact Christian friends* from your area and invite them to join your training group. Share what you have already learned. Keep at it, until you find at least one new person willing to join the group.

2. *Deliver a copy of* WITNESS, as soon as possible, to those who have agreed to come with you to the group, so they can read the lecture they missed and do the homework in order to catch up. (No one will be able to join your group after the second meeting.)

3. *Arrange to come with your friend* to the group, so he will not feel ill at ease entering into a new situation. Transportation, baby sitters, etc., may be problems you can help him solve, to enable him to join the group.

4. *Learn from your act of invitation.* Some will say "No," others "Yes." Both are valuable experiences from which to learn and will stand you in good stead later on when you invite other friends to the Outreach Groups. Next week, you will have the chance to discuss with the group your experience of trying to invite others.

The Spontaneous Missionary Church

By Prof. Hans-Ruedi Weber

Christ sent forth His apostles to herald the Gospel to the whole inhabited world and to do so until the close of the ages. The apostles obeyed, particularly the one who called himself "the least of the apostles," Paul. But surprisingly enough, Paul and the others apparently did little to spur Christians to herald the Gospel in their pagan environment. No evangelizing campaigns, no mission boards, and even little, if any, organized missionary activity. And yet, the Church was constantly growing. The apostles died — and the Church continued to grow!

THE CLOUD OF UNKNOWN WITNESSES

We do well to learn the lesson of these early centuries which were one of the most fruitful periods in the history of missions and which in many ways can be compared with ours.

Origen gives us the following picture of mid-third-century conditions: "Christians do all in their power to spread the faith over the world. Some of them therefore make it their business in life to wander not only from city to city but even to villages and hamlets, to win fresh converts for the Lord." Most of these itinerant teachers were laymen, far more comparable to the Christian "sadhu" in India and the Christian "guru" in Indonesia than to any modern missionary. The missionary expansion depended on movements of spontaneous enthusiasm. The main work was done by the cloud of unknown witnesses, the Christian tradesmen and artisans, the soldiers and slaves and, last but not least, the Christian women.

Celsus, the great enemy of the Christian Church in the second century, gives a disdainful caricature of the little people who, ever ready for a martyr's death, brought the Gospel into the recesses of society: "We see in private houses, workers in wool and leather, washermen, and persons of the most uneducated and rustic kind. They would not venture to open their mouth in the presence of their elders or their wiser masters. But they get hold of the children privately and any women who are as ignorant as themselves. Then they pour out wonderful statements: 'You ought not to heed your father, or your teachers. Obey us. They are foolish and stupid, neither know nor can do anything really good, being busied with empty trifles. We alone know how men ought to live. If your children do as we say, you will be happy yourselves and make your home happy also!' While they are speaking, they see one of the school teachers approaching, or one of the more educated class, or even the father himself. . . . So they whisper, 'With him here we can't explain . . . but if you like, you can come with the women and your play-mates to the women's quarters or the leathershop or the laundry that you may get all there is.' With words like these, they win them over."

The great test is whether "the wonderful statements" of these cobblers and laundry workers were mere words or whether they could point to the reality of Christ's power. The ancient Church surely passed the test. For it can be said not only about the apostles but also about these little men and women: "They went out and preached that men should repent, and they cast out devils" (Mark 6:12-13). Origen testifies: "Not a few Christians exorcise sufferers and that without manipulations and magic or the use of drugs, but just by prayer and an invocation of the simpler kind, and such means as the simpler kind of man might be able to use. For it is mostly people quite untrained who do this work."

But the early Christians had still more to point to than these exorcisms which are rather strange for sophisticated Christians of the West (and not at all strange for members of the so-called younger churches). The astonishing Christian community life and the Christian service — in ecumenical slogans we would say: the "koinonia" and the "diakonia" — gave the necessary sounding board for the spoken message to become real proclamation instead of being empty declamation. The pagan satirist Lucian of the second century testified: "Their first legislator succeeded in convincing them that they were all brothers; they show incredible activity as soon as anything happens which affects their communal interests; they consider no price too dear to protect them" — And Tertullian wrote the following famous words: "Our care for people who cannot help themselves, our works of charity, have become a distinguishing mark by which our enemies recognize us: 'See how these Christians love one another,' they say (for they themselves hate one another) 'and how one Christian is ready to die for another!' (whereas they themselves would be more prepared to destroy each other)."

Commenting on this ministering community life of the early Christians, A. Harnack exclaimed: "What a sense of stability a creation of this kind must have conferred upon the individual! What powers of attraction it must have exercised, as soon as its object came to be understood! It was this, and not any evangelist, which proved to be the most effective missionary. In fact, we may take it as an assured fact that the mere existence and persistent activity of the individual Christian communities did more than anything else to bring about the extension of the Christian religion."

A CLUE TO THE RIDDLE OF SPONTANEOUS WITNESS

What was the source of this spontaneous witness? The first and obvious clue to this riddle is of course the power of the Holy Spirit. We will come back to it. But there is another, closely related clue which can be illustrated by a parallel development of spontaneous missionary outreach: the expansion of Islam.

It has been said that the explanation of the continuing missionary expansion of Islam is what to non-Moslems seems to be a superiority complex: the strong consciousness of Moslems to be the one elect and privileged "umma," the one and only true community of God. Allah claims the whole world. All the areas which do not yet fall under the Moslem theocracy are therefore "areas of the war," where the true worship has to be introduced whether by force or persuasion. Every Moslem, kindled by such a self-consciousness, becomes spontaneously a propagandist, mainly Moslem tradesmen and colonists. The same thing happens today in West Africa.

Granted all the differences between Islam and the Christian faith and therefore the quite different nature and exigencies of Moslem propaganda and Christian missions, there is here a revealing parallel: Christians also have such a particular self-consciousness, the consciousness of being "the people," the "laos," i.e., "a chosen race, a royal priesthood, a holy nation, God's own people" (I Peter 2:9). If this self-consciousness is not embedded in an equally strong knowledge that we are God's people solely by the mercy of God, such a faith becomes intolerably arrogant. We know it from certain missionary practices not only of Moslem and Christian sects, but also of respectable Christian churches! Yet, whether arrogant or not, such a self-consciousness is a strong missionary drive. It surely was in the ancient Church.

This self-consciousness of early Christians has found a most beautiful expression in the much quoted letter to Diognetus (in the second or third century): "Christians cannot be distinguished from the rest of the human race by country or language or customs. They do not live in cities of their own; they do not use a peculiar form of speech; they do not follow an eccentric manner of life. . . . Yet, although they live in Greek and barbarian cities alike, as each man's lot has been cast, and follow the customs of the country in clothing and food and other matters of daily living, at the same time they give proof of the remarkable and admittedly extraordinary constitution of their commonwealth. They live in their own countries, but as aliens. They have a share in everything as citizens, and endure everything as foreigners. Every foreign land is their fatherland, and yet for them every fatherland is a foreign land. . . . They busy themselves on earth, but their citizenship is in heaven. To put it simply: what the soul is in the body, the Christians are in the world."

This consciousness of being God's own people which became such a vital missionary drive, was intimately related to the early Christians' understanding of what happened in baptism and confirmation. Besides the forgiveness of sin, the reception of the Holy Spirit, etc., baptism was also considered as a military oath. By becoming a Christian, by the "sacramentum," the baptismal vows, we cease to be civilians and we all become soldiers actively engaged in Christ's struggle for the world. The New Testament and the early Church never admitted a distinction between active and passive members. Every one was a missionary. And every baptized person had the authority to be a missionary. For baptism and the accompanying unction were also considered as some kind of an ordination.

TOWARD A SPONTANEOUS MISSIONARY CHURCH

It would be futile to try to copy the spontaneous mission of the ancient Church. But we may at least try to learn a lesson.

1. One of the clues to the spontaneous mission of the ancient Church was the *strong consciousness of being God's own peculiar people*. It is no secret that this biblical self-consciousness of Christians has faded away, especially among the more respectable churches and where a church finds itself in a majority church situation.

2. In the ancient Church the "laos-consciousness" was intimately related to *baptism and confirmation*.

3. The ancient church considered the unction which accompanied baptism as an indelible "ordination" as prophet, priest and king.

4. Spontaneous witness has much to do with holy living, or, more accurately, with *holy worldliness* — and one cannot escape the impression that the early Christians did not only call themselves "saints" but that they really were saints. Of course, not such sugary or inhuman saints with a halo. One has only to read Paul's letter to the "saints" in Corinth to know better. But to be a Christian made a difference. The already

quoted testimonies of the first three centuries are unanimous in this respect.

5. Paul wrote to the Ephesians that it is the specific function of apostles, prophets, evangelists, pastors and teachers, "to equip the saints for the work of ministry."

6. The spontaneous mission of the ancient Church teaches us to *broaden our conception of missions and evangelism.* The specific function of missionaries and evangelists is not to fulfil the Church's missionary and evangelistic task but rather to animate, equip and guide the saints in their missionary and evangelistic living, action and proclamation.

7. When trying to learn the lesson of ancient church history with regard to the spontaneous outreach of the Church, one must mention the books of Roland Allen. The main concern and message of the prophet Roland Allen is as timely today as ever: *his call to trust the Holy Spirit.* The very heart of spontaneous mission is this trust in the power of the Holy Spirit. "I venture to insist that missionaries of the Gospel have only one proper activity, the ministration of the Spirit of Christ." And this "ministration of the Spirit speaks not of what *we* (the missionaries) can do, but of what *they* (the converts) can do in the power of the Spirit. We missionaries find it extremely hard to appreciate this mighty manifestation of the Spirit, because a change which is clearly visible to a man's heathen neighbours and friends is often wholly invisible to us. Therefore we continue our great organized missionary and evangelistic activities. Result: all the little everyday missionary living, service and speaking of simple laymen and laywomen is overshadowed by the comparatively great organized activities of the committees. They get the idea that the only proper way to do Christian work is to join a preaching band, or to support a great organization by contributions. . . . The force of simple daily activities is lost to them. . . ."*

*Adapted from *Laity* Magazine, pp. 72-85; Volume 4; May, 1962 by permission of Prof. Weber.

Bibliography

A. PERSONAL WITNESS

**1. *You Can Witness With Confidence* by Rosalind Rinker; Zondervan Publishing House.

One of the best introductory books on the subject of Christian witness. Sane, simple, interesting and practical, this is one book you ought to study thoroughly.

*2. *How to Give Away Your Faith* by Paul Little; IVCF Press.

A highly amusing yet perceptive study of witnessing written by a man engaged in student evangelism. There is a splendid chapter on the reasons which lie behind our faith.

B. EVANGELISM

**1. *The Christian Persuader* by Leighton Ford; Hodder and Stoughton.

An up-to-date look at evangelism written by an evangelist who is well aware of the problems of today's world.

*2. *What Is Evangelism?* by Douglas Webster; The Highway Press.

This study treats the types of outsiders we seek to reach, ways of reaching them, and their subsequent experience of conversion.

3. *Missionary Methods: St. Paul's or Ours?; The Ministry of the Spirit;* and *The Spontaneous Expansion of the Church;* by Roland Allen; Wm. B. Eerdmans Publishing Co.

Classic studies of methods of outreach (referred to by H. R. Weber in the Supplementary Reading).

C. ROLE OF LAITY

**1. *Dedication and Leadership: Learning from the Communists* by Douglas Hyde; Notre Dame Press.

A study of how the Communists train and then use individuals to propagate their message, with lessons for the Church pointed out. This is a fascinating and deeply relevant book.

2. *A Theology of the Laity* by Hendrik Kraemer, Lutterworth; *God's Frozen People* by Morton and Gibbs, Fontana; and *We the People* by Kathleen Bliss, SCM Press.

Three volumes which discuss the often misunderstood role of the lay person in the work of the Church.

3. *Revolution in Evangelism* by W. Dayton Roberts; Scripture Union and *Evangelism in Depth;* Moody Press.

The exciting story of the mobilization of the laity for evangelism in Latin America.

Please note that an * before a book indicates the best books (in my judgment) on each subject. I have marked a few books **. These are books which I feel everyone should read and master if at all possible.

Chapter 2

The Problems of Witness

The Problems of Witness

Group Exercises

PHASE I: *The Experience of Inviting Others* (30 minutes).

Last week, each person sought to invite at least one Christian friend to join the training group. Hence, in this session, you either:

(a)   Had the experience of inviting others; or

(b)   You were invited.

We now want to see what we can learn from this experience. Below are several questions. Think about these for the next three minutes. You can make notes if necessary. Then the group will discuss them.

Answer these questions if you *invited others*:

1.   What success did you have?

2.   How did you go about inviting people?

3.   What reasons did people give for joining the group? For not joining?

4.   What problems had to be overcome before people were free to join?

5. Did you enjoy inviting others? Why, or why not?

6. What did you learn about *motives* (i.e. about what induces a person to act) — your own and that of other people — in the whole experience?

Answer these questions if you *were invited*:

1. What was your first reaction to the invitation?

2. What made you decide to come?

3. Were there any factors which almost prevented you from coming?

PHASE II: *The Lecture* (13 minutes).

As you listen to the lecture, make a list of the problems which hinder Christians from witnessing. Include in this list as well, points which occur to you, but which may not necessarily have been mentioned in the lecture.

Reasons for not witnessing	*Ways to overcome these*
1.	
2.	
3.	

4. _____ _____

5. _____ _____

6. _____ _____

7. _____ _____

8. _____ _____

9. _____ _____

10. _____ _____

11. _____ _____

12. _____ _____

13. _____ _____

14. _____ _____

15. _____ _____

PHASE III: *The Witnessing Community* (45 minutes).

Below is a passage from the Acts of the Apostles which tells of an incident in the life of the early Church. We are going to study this passage because herein are certain clues as to the source of the great power which the New Testament Church possessed. This group is the *model of what a witnessing community should be.*

This incident is preceded by the arrest of Peter and John for preaching about Jesus in the Temple after they had healed a lame man. They are taken before the Jewish political and religious leaders (the same ones who had put Jesus to death) and ordered "bluntly not to speak or teach a single further word about the name of Jesus." (vs. 18). They refuse, point blank, to abide by this order! Our passage begins as Peter and John return to the group of believers:

> *After their release the apostles went back to their friends and reported to them what the chief priests and Elders had said to them. When they heard it they raised their voices to God in united prayer and said,*

"Almighty Lord, thou art the one who hast made the heaven and the earth, the sea and all that is in them . . . In this city the rulers have gathered together against thy holy servant, Jesus, thine anointed — yes, Herod and Pontius Pilate, the Gentiles and the peoples of Israel have gathered together to carry out what thine hand and will had planned to happen. And now, O Lord, observe their threats and give thy servants courage to speak thy Word fearlessly, while thou dost stretch out thine hand to heal, and cause signs and wonders to be performed in the name of thy holy servant Jesus."

When they had prayed their meeting-place was shaken; they were all filled with the Holy Spirit and spoke the Word of God fearlessly.

Among the large number who had become believers there was a complete agreement of heart and soul. Not one of them claimed any of his possessions as his own but everything was common property to all. The apostles continued to give their witness to the Resurrection of the Lord Jesus with great force, and a wonderful spirit of generosity pervaded the whole fellowship. Indeed, there was not a single person in need among them, for those who owned land or property would sell it and bring the proceeds of the sales and place it at the apostles' feet. They distributed to each one according to his need.

(Acts 4:23-35; Phillips Translation.)

1. Go back over this passage now, and make a list of *the characteristics of the group*. What was the group like? (Take eight minutes to answer this and the next two questions.)

2. Now list the different factors that *motivated* this group to witness.

3. What can we learn of value for the present-day Church from the characteristics and motivation of this first-century Church?

Study Schedule

READ:

1. *The Text of the Lecture,* asking yourself, "Which are my problems and what can I do about them?"

2. *The Supplementary Paper,* "The Tyranny of the Urgent" in which the time problem is faced.

3. *Sections from those books in the Bibliography* which deal with aspects of this lecture which especially puzzle or interest you.

4. *Extra Reading* (if you have time), entitled "What Non-Christians Ask" by Paul Little in which he outlines approaches to some of the intellectual problems of Christianity, found in Appendix A.

CONSIDER FOR YOURSELF:

"Witnessing and Me," in such a way as to identify what your problems in witnessing actually are.

ACT:

By trying consciously to overcome one of the hindrances you have in witnessing, discussing with another person, both the problem and what you are doing about it.

The Problems in Witnessing

"You have never found any problems in being a witness? You have never witnessed!"

We are all called to be witnesses for Christ. We are called to say to this desperate world: "In Christ is what you seek." The task is ours.

But when we are honest, we must admit that most of us have done a pretty poor job as witnesses. We have to face this. It is nothing to be ashamed of nor feel guilty about. Nor must we feel as if we alone have failed. There are very few, if any of us, who have never had problems in being faithful and effective witnesses for Christ.

However, before we can overcome those things that prevent us from being witnesses, we have got to stop and become aware of what our problems are. Once we can *admit* we are hindered as witnesses and can *identify* specifically what it is that binds us, then we are in a position to do something about the problem. In fact, it is often found that facing and naming the problem is 90 percent of the solution.

So if we are serious about assuming our role in the work of evangelism and outreach, the place we must begin is with our past failures. Perhaps the best way of coming to grips with our particular problems is by examining some of the common hindrances which other Christians have known.

FEARS

If I were asked to name the most common hindrance to witness I would say that it was fear. However, fear takes various shapes and forms in the experience of different people.

1. *What Will I Say?*

For example, many people fear that if they seek to share their faith with others, *they simply will not know what to say*. Perhaps at some point they have tried to talk about Christianity and found that they could not find the right words easily. They know they believe. They know, in a general way, what they believe. But putting this into words — into clear, concise sentences — is more than they can cope with.

Let me admit at this point that such a fear is a real one. It is not to be minimized. We ought to be concerned if we cannot articulate our faith. But let me also hasten to add that we *can* learn to do this. In fact, it is not difficult to learn how to express the meaning of Christianity to others. The problem is that few of us have ever had the opportunity to sit down and try to put into words what we believe; and then to discuss what we have done with other Christians. Yet this is really the only way to learn.

You will have such an opportunity in this Training Course. If you have looked ahead in the Manual you will see that two sessions (a quarter of the entire course) are devoted to this very subject — learning to speak about our faith. So if your fear in witnessing is over your inability to articulate the meaning of Christianity, be assured that you can learn, and that this course will give you the opportunity to do so.

2. *How Will I Answer?*

Some people, however, have developed a certain facility in discussing the fundamental aspects of Christianity — but they are still bound by the fear that if they get into a conversation about Christianity, they *will not be able to answer all the questions that might be asked.* "And," so they reason, "if I can't do that I might as well be silent lest I make a mess of it."

This is largely a needless fear, however. For one thing, it is quite true that most of us will *not* be able to answer every possible query about Christianity. But then few people — minister or layman — could! In any case, no one expects us to have an encyclopedic knowledge of Christianity. When we become Christians we do not automatically become mini-theologians. Our knowledge of Christianity grows over the years. In such situations in which we are asked questions which we cannot answer, our duty is simply to say; "I don't know." We can, of course, offer to try and find out the answer. Answers do exist. But what counts most in such situations is honesty, not total knowledge.[1]

On the other hand, we *do* know certain things. And it is what we know that we are called upon to share. What we know about the fundamental areas of Christianity is the important thing, not what we do not know about esoteric philosophical arguments.

However, this is not to say we should be unconcerned about objections to Christianity. An excellent starting point for you in thinking these through is the article entitled "What Non-Christians Ask," by Paul Little, which is reprinted in the Appendix. Quite apart from anything else, if you begin to master this material, you will develop a new confidence in witness as you come to realize that Christianity is not mere fairy-tale, but has solid historical foundations, which can be investigated by any fair inquirer.

3. *Will I Offend?*

A third fear which hinders many of us from sharing our faith is the *fear of offending others.* We fear, for example, that if we broach the subject of Christianity with our neighbor, we will put him off because "as everyone knows there are two things which should not be discussed — politics and religion."

But will people be put off if we talk about Christ? They will if we hammer them. I once knew a chap who relentlessly hammered people with the Gospel. One of the things which John (let us call him that) did was to carry everywhere a specially fitted-out briefcase. Inside were literally hundreds of leaflets covering a multitude of subjects, neatly arranged in pockets. When John met a new person, he almost inevitably at some point snapped open his case and whipped a leaflet into the person's unsuspecting hand. He coupled this with the admonition: "This is just what you need. Read it."

John had leaflets to fit every occasion. If he saw a person smoking, he would issue a leaflet on the evils of this habit.

If he felt a person's behavior was suspect, he gave him a leaflet about repentance and judgment. I once received a leaflet because he caught me carrying a copy of Thomas Kempis' *Imitation of Christ*. The leaflet informed me, in no uncertain terms, that a real Christian ought not to read any religious books save the Bible!

John did offend people — not by daring to discuss Christianity, but rather by the way he went about it; by his rudeness, by his judgmental attitude, and by his lack of love. When several of us spoke to John about this on one occasion his reply was: "We are told in the Bible to expect that the Gospel will be an offense to many." What John could not see was that *he personally* was the offense, not the Gospel. In fact, he offended people so deeply that they never even heard the Gospel from him.

You will find, in actual fact, that most people are not put off by a discussion concerning Christianity. Over and over again I have been surprised at how eager people are to talk about Christ. Far from offending others by speaking of Christ, we often open to them a topic in which they are deeply interested.

4. *What If I Fail?*

A fourth fear is the *fear of failure*. Many Christians reason like this: "It is really not worth while for me to try to be a witness. After all, I never seem to be able to interest anyone in Christianity. I'll just have to leave it to those who can succeed."

There are several problems in this sort of reasoning. For one thing, we are *all* called to witness — not just those who happen to be articulate or skillful. We cannot just "leave it to someone else" and still be faithful to the Christ we follow.

An even deeper problem, however, comes when we reason that if we are not successful as witnesses, we might as well give up. Is this so? Must we stop witnessing unless we see most of those to whom we speak actually become Christians? No, our mandate is simply to *share our faith*. "Preach the Gospel," Christ said. He did not say that we must make sure that everyone to whom we preach the Gospel responds positively. Results are God's concern. We must not be paralyzed by the fear that others might not receive what we say in the way we would like them to receive it.

It is interesting to note that in the one place in which our Lord does comment on success and failure in outreach (Mark 4 — the parable of the Sower) three types of *failure* are listed before success is recorded. Our job is to sow the seed of the Word of God. It is God who brings the increase.

Of course we cannot use this as an excuse either. If we faithfully share our faith, we will see results eventually. As one man has put it: ". . . fishers of men are meant to *catch* men, not just to influence them. What should we think of an angler who said: 'How many fish have I caught? Oh, I haven't *caught* any, but I've *influenced* quite a few'."[2]

5. Will I Be a Hypocrite?

Perhaps the biggest fear of all for many people is the *fear of hypocrisy.* "How can I tell others about something of which I am unsure myself?"

For some, this problem arises because there is a fundamental uncertainty about their own relationship to Jesus Christ. It is easy to grow up in a church (or drift into one). It is easy to be pleased with the organization, to find friends there, to support its ideals and programs — and yet all the time fail to come to grips with the essential issue of who Jesus Christ is and what our relationship to Him is meant to be.

Fundamentally, Christianity is all about a relationship with Jesus Christ. Christianity is not basically an ethic, an ideology, a set of doctrines, a particular view of life or an organization. It involves all of these aspects — but each of these grows out of the vital ongoing relationship between the individual and Jesus Christ. To attempt to make any of these other aspects fundamental is to rob Christianity of its essence and to doom ourselves to ultimate disillusionment. Christianity will not work without Christ at the core.

So too in witnessing. It will not work if our witness is about the superior moral code of Christianity; or about what a great minister we have; or about all the good things our church is doing for others. All these issues can and should enter into our total witness, but always in the context of the fundamental issue of who Jesus is.

Hence this is the fundamental issue for us too. We *ought* to have a fear of witness if we ourselves have yet to resolve this issue of whether or not we are serious about opening our lives to the living Christ in such a way that He becomes the center of our existence. We cannot really speak to others about Christianity in any power or depth until we have come to grips with and resolved this issue for ourselves. We cannot talk about Christ until we have met Christ.

6. *What If Christ Seems Distant?*

The fear of hypocrisy can take other forms too. For example, a person may in fact have become a real Christian at some point in his life. And yet, his Christian experience seems so unreal at times. So he reasons: "How can I speak to others about Christ when He seems distant to me? I would be a hypocrite."

If Christ is distant, there are reasons. Most often it is because we have drifted away from His influence. Because of the pressures of our busy life, we have neglected all but minimal contact with Christ. We do not pray. We spend little time in meaningful dialogue with others who are also striving to follow Christ. We seldom do any serious study of Scripture. We never stop and meditate on the course our life is taking. Of course Christ seems distant!

If we are honest, there are few of us for whom this is an alien experience. All of us know what it means to drift imperceptibly away from any real influence of Christ — until one day we are jolted into the awareness that the vitality of our faith has diminished markedly.

At such a point, we ought not to allow feelings of guilt to paralyze us into inaction. What we must do is to take steps to remedy the situation. *The first thing we must do is to win the battle of time.* We will not know Christ in any depth until we start spending time with Him. We have to set aside a definite period each day during which we consciously seek to know God's mind. It need not be long. Fifteen minutes a day will serve as a start.

Then secondly, we have got to use this time for Bible study, prayer and meditation. *In the Bible* we get insight into ourselves, into Christ and into the world. We literally "hear God's word" there. The Bible is also the standard by which we judge our life. *In prayer* we simply talk to Christ — about the real issues we face, about the problems we have, and about the joys we know. And then *in meditation* we draw all this together. In the light of what we have read and said, we consider our life at that moment, and seek to know God's direction for it.

Thirdly, coupled with this seeking of Christ on an individual level there ought to be a seeking of Him in fellowship with others. We really do need one another in this. This is why the Church was created — as a fellowship of followers, learning together to know Christ, ministering to one another.

When we seek to know Christ individually and in community, we will, in fact, find Him. And as the sense of His power and presence grows, so too will the depth and reality of our witness to others.

One more note, however. Even when we are obeying the rules of relationship with Christ, there come those times of barrenness, when God seems far away. Our prayers rebound from the ceiling. The Bible is dry and without life.

Do realize that this is not an unusual experience. Saints throughout the ages testify to it. But they also say in retrospect, (and this is the important thing), that when God seems most distant they have found that in fact He was the closest. They find that in such times of dryness they have learned deep and rich lessons. Furthermore, they testify that such periods do not last forever.

But how can we *witness* when we are unaware of the reality of Christ? The answer is — the same way we witness any other time: by reflecting honestly what we know of Christ and not pretending to be what we are not. It is strange, but often in the times of greatest weakness, we have the most impact upon others.

For example, a minister friend told me of an experience he once had. He had been invited to conduct a "Memorial Service for the British War Dead." He had accepted the invitation, duly entered it into his diary, and even prepared a sermon months in advance. But then, without being aware of it, he accepted a second invitation for the same day and time. When the time came my friend was at his other appointment — while the Mayor and other officials sat waiting at the Memorial Service. Fortunately another minister who happened to be present stepped in and took the service.

Shortly thereafter a letter appeared in the newspaper berating the "callousness of ministers who did not bother to turn up at functions." My friend wrote back to the newspaper saying: "Lest there be any misunderstanding about which minister did not turn up, let me say that I am the guilty one." He then offered his apologies.

He was somewhat fearful about the result of this public confession. However, he found to his surprise that it seemed to produce a new openness and freedom in his church! Even the minister could fail, the people discovered. So the members of the congregation were far more able to confess their own failure — and thus come to grips with it. The point is this: our very failure can, in fact, be a source of positive witness.

7. Can I Witness When I Am So Imperfect?

This brings up yet another aspect of this fear of hypocrisy. Some people say: "I can't witness about Christ. Who am I to speak? I'm so imperfect." Of course you are. We all are. This is the point. We are all men and women with deep needs and problems, who have come to Christ with these very needs and are finding in Him the answer to them. When we decide to follow Christ, we do not instantly become perfect. But we *are* growing. We *are* beginning to cope. And as we look back over the years we can see progress which has been made in our lives.

Yet sometimes we are trapped into believing that we have to be perfect before we can speak. However, what intrigues the non-Christian is discovering an imperfect person (like himself) with real problems (as he has) coping with these in the awesome power of Christ.

As someone has said: "Don't wait to witness until you are perfect. Witnessing involves being honest all the time — now. Never cover up your weaknesses in order to witness. What the world is waiting to see is not a perfect Christian, but the miracle of grace working in a weak, imperfect Christian."[3]

SENSE OF INSUFFICIENCY

Not only are we hindered in our witness by our fears, but we are also hindered by our sense of insufficiency. "I would witness, if only I had the time, or if I had the motivation, or if I had the faith." We feel that if we could gain these elusive elements — time, motivation, or faith — *then* we would be a witness.

1. Insufficient Time

Take the matter of time. I have seldom met a person (at least from a Western culture) who felt he had time to spare. We all consider ourselves to be busy people. And we are. Our days are full — and we do not see how we can take on another thing. And yet, *we are able to meet unexpected demands on our time.* For example, a friend phones and says he has tickets for Saturday's football game. We need no persuading to accompany him. And yet, on Saturday we had planned to start painting the spare bedroom. But it can wait. . . . And so it goes. When we think about it, it really is not a question of "no available time" is it? It is basically a question of priorities. *We do what we want to do.* We are able to make time for whatever grips us.

It would be an interesting (though disconcerting!) experiment to keep track of how we in fact spend our time during an average week. To do this, make a list, beginning with the moment you rise in the morning. How long does dressing and eating take? How is the middle of your day spent? Where does the time go after 5:00 p.m.? What about the evenings? The week-ends? One friend, when he did this, was horrified to discover how much time he spent at sports. Another discovered that he averaged two hours a day gardening.

Now neither gardening nor sports is wrong, but the question remains: "Is the amount of time we spend on these activities out of proportion, especially when compared to the time we devote to what we *say* is most important to us?"

2. *Insufficient Motivation*

This brings us quite naturally to the whole subject of motivation. The problem of time is really a problem of motivation. If we are motivated, we will find the time to do quite a lot. But so often we are not motivated as Christians to share our faith with others. Why is this? We have a message which is true. We have a message which this world desperately needs. And yet when one compares the motivation level of the average Christian to the motivation level of the average Communist, the comparison is devastating.

What ought to motivate us to witness? One thing is our Lord's command. A common Biblical image of the Christian life is that of warfare. When we decide to follow Christ, we join Christ's army. Our role then is as a faithful soldier. Hence when our Commander-in-Chief says: "Go share the Gospel with everyone," we do so. It is a response of obedience.

This is a legitimate motivation, but it is still external. That is, it is a commandment which comes from outside ourselves. A deeper and more powerful motivation is that which arises out of the richness of our personal experience of Christ. "I know Christ's love and hence I cannot help but tell others." This again points up the need we have to develop our relationship with Christ.

3. *Insufficient Faith*

However, I do not think we have yet got to the root of the motivation problem. Quite frankly, for me, the problem of motivation was really a problem of faith. For a long while that which most deeply hindered my witness was the uncertainty I felt as to whether Christ was indeed the answer to everyone's need. He was the answer to my needs. I believed this. I experienced this. Yet when I was honest, I knew that there was a core of uncertainty within me when it came to others. I was not sure they also needed Him.

I could look at the confident young man with the expensive suit, beautiful girl friend, fast sports car and excellent job. *Here is a man who has no needs at all,* I thought. *He has it made. He probably does not need Christ.*

I only began to cope with this problem of unbelief when I started to see beneath surface appearances. It was a major revelation for me to discover that everyone wears a mask over his true self, revealing only a carefully chosen "image" in public. But beneath the mask, at the point of our real self, deep needs reside — inner loneliness, quiet desperation, lack of motivation, fears, guilt, uncertainty. *And we are all like this.* No one is exempt. Needs are part of human nature. Hence we all need Christ. I believe that any effort at witness will be half-hearted until the issue is solved of whether we feel other people do in fact need Christ.

How does one cope with this sense of unbelief? I can give no easy answer, except to say that you must investigate this issue on several levels. For one thing, you must ask yourself the key question: "Do I really believe that Christ is the unique Son of God, the one whose life, death and resurrection opened up for man the possibility of knowing God?" You must allow your *mind* to be persuaded that Christianity is true and that Christ is who He claimed to be.

But once your mind is convinced, then your emotions must also be persuaded. You must "know" within yourself the reality of need within your fellow man. This is an awareness which grows as we grow in Christ. It is an awareness which, in some senses, only God Himself can give us. If this is your problem perhaps you ought to pray for the vision to see people as they really are.

The Problems of Witness

For some of us, it is not fear and it is not a sense of insufficiency which hinders us in our witness. Rather, it is a misunderstanding of what evangelism and witness is all about.

1. *Misunderstanding Evangelism*

Take this whole matter of evangelism for a moment. A lot of sincere Christians are highly dubious about the value of evangelism. The reason for this is that to them evangelism is associated with emotionalism, exploitation of people, tearful confessions, hypocrisy and high-pressure. Their image of an evangelistic meeting is a cross between a high-powered political rally and the circus. No wonder that for some "evangelism" has almost become a theological swear word.

Unfortunately, these images have some basis in fact. During a certain era many abuses were perpetrated in the name of evangelism. Even though that era is mercifully past, its image still haunts us.

However, such abuses were never really evangelism, simply because the essence of evangelism is not a peculiar method, but a particular message. Evangelism is not a technique but a message — a message about Christ's life, death and resurrection. The forms and methods through which this message is presented can vary widely.

So do not be put off evangelism because in your mind it is associated with certain *methods* with which you cannot identify. Evangelism is essentially a message — a message which every generation must strive to present in ways that will commend it to the hearers.

Others are putting off evangelism because they feel that it is irrelevant to what they call the "real issues" in the world today — such as hunger, racial hatred and war. Once again, I must say that in some instances this charge is accurate. Some Christians have felt that their duty to the world was fulfilled by sitting in a seat at an evangelistic rally. Being so concerned about the spiritual needs of their neighbor they forgot about his physical needs.

But this is not the Biblical pattern. St. James has stern words for such people:

> If a fellow man or woman has no clothes to wear and nothing to eat, and one of you say, "Good luck to you, I hope you'll keep warm and find enough to eat," and yet give them nothing to meet their physical needs, what on earth is the good of that?[4]

Our Lord combined in His own ministry a concern for the physical (remember those 5,000 He fed?) with a concern for the spiritual (His first words in Mark's Gospel were: "Repent and believe in the Gospel").[5] He saw men as whole beings, with both physical and spiritual needs. To avoid meeting either need is to be unfaithful to the wholeness of the Gospel. True evangelism must reflect this.

Both emphases are needed. You see, it has often been said that the reason there are so many social problems is that "not enough people care." True enough. But often people do not care because they cannot care. Their own problems are so deep and so consuming that they can only be concerned about themselves. Such people can begin to care only when they start to cope with these personal needs. This becomes possible when they find new life in Christ. Evangelism is therefore the foundation for social concern, in that by finding Christ, individuals are freed enough from their own needs to be able to reach out to meet the needs of others — if they are given the opportunity. The dichotomy between evangelism and social concern is a false one.

2. *Misunderstanding Witness*

Likewise, do not be put off personal *witness* because of a certain caricature you have of what a Christian witness is. A lot of us recoil from the grab-them-by-the-necktie and hammer-them-with-the-Gospel approach. Hence we are hindered in becoming witnesses because we think this is what is required — and we just cannot do it.

But this is not witness. Once again the error comes in defining witness as a peculiar method, when really it is a message.

Witness is not essentially a technique. At its core *witnessing is just being honest as a Christian*. It is not saying certain things in certain ways in order to elicit certain responses. It is sharing Christ honestly and openly, in all naturalness.

> To let your light shine demands no more than honesty. It demands honesty before unbelievers. In fact honesty is in itself 90 percent of witnessing. Witnessing is not putting on a Christian front so as to convince prospective customers. Witnessing is being honest, that is, being true to what God has made you in your speech and in your day by day behaviour. . . . If you are partially honest (total honesty is rare and difficult) in a conversation with an unbeliever, you will find it difficult to avoid talking about Christian things.[6]

This concept of witnessing as being honest, is utterly fundamental. So we will be returning to it again and again in this course. At this point, suffice it to say that if you are hindered in your witness because you believe it involves certain "techniques," rest assured that this is not so. The deepest and finest witness occurs when we are the most transparently open to others — allowing them to see and to hear Christ through us. Our problem is that most of us go to great lengths to avoid even mentioning Christ!

Witnessing and Me

Few of us are a consistent verbal witness for Christ because we are hindered in one way or another.

As we strive to become witnesses, we must come to the point where we face up to our particular hindrances, and then decide how to cope with them.

Read through the following questions slowly and meditatively. In questions 1 and 4, check those answers which you feel describe your own reactions.

1. I seldom talk about Christ with others because:
   (a) I am afraid I will offend if I do ....
   (b) I really don't know what I would say if I tried to talk to another person. ....
   (c) I feel this isn't my job to talk about Christ with others ....
   (d) If I did get into discussion I just know I would be unable to answer questions which might be asked ....
   (e) I guess, when you get right down to it, I'm not terribly sure my friends need Christ ....
   (f) I have seen Christians "witnessing" to others, and I would be terribly embarrassed to do that sort of thing ....
   (g) I'm afraid I'm not sure whether I could say I have any sort of vital relationship with Christ ....
   (h) Though I do know Christ, I fear I seldom experience His power and influence in my life ....
   (i) I am afraid others won't accept what I say ....
   (j) I don't want to be a hypocrite ....
   (k) I am just not motivated to witness ....
   (l) Other reasons _____

2. This being the case, I feel I can best cope with my particular problems by:

_____

_____

_____

3. In the days to come, I am going to be particularly sensitive to natural opportunities which arise in which I can speak about Christ. Such opportunities will probably come up in my conversation with the following people:

_____

_____

_____

4. I am reticent to get involved in any organized evangelistic effort because:
   (a) I don't have the time _____
       (As I evaluate how I use my time, I believe I could get more involved if I changed my timetable as follows: _____

_____

_____)

   (b) I just don't like "evangelism" and am hesitant to be associated with such endeavors _____
       (What I dislike about evangelism is _____

_____

_____

_____)

Lord, You know me so well. You know all the excuses I use to avoid talking about You with others. I present these excuses to You now. Help me to become free and natural as I talk about You. May I know

Your power in my life so that when I speak it will be out of a vital relationship with You.

Lord, Your very weak and inadequate servant now offers to You what talents he has. Use them far beyond my expectation. Make my experience of sharing You with others a joyous one.

Amen.

1. *Pick one particular problem* which you face in witnessing, on the basis of what you wrote in "Witnessing and Me," and

2. *Try to begin to overcome this problem* this week.

    For example, your problem may be that of unbelief — you just cannot believe all your friends need Christ. You can meet this by: *praying* that God will give you insight into the real needs of people; *reading Scripture* to see what it has to say; and perhaps *discussing* with a friend your feelings at this point.

    Or, your problem may be the fear of offending others. You can meet this by casually mentioning to the chap at the next desk that you are getting involved in this training course — and see what happens. You will find, I am sure, that far from being offended, he will be interested.

3. *Share this problem* with someone else and discuss what you have done to overcome it. Get advice and help from another person. A telephone call to another member of your group will probably be the easiest way to do this.

The Problems of Witness

Tyranny of the Urgent

By Charles Hummel

Christ's three-year-old ministry seems too short in retrospect. A prostitute at Simon's banquet found forgiveness, but how many others walked the street? For every ten withered muscles that had flexed into health, a hundred remained impotent. Jesus healed hundreds but thousands remained ill. How then could He say at the end of a short life: "I have finished the work which Thou gavest me to do" (John 17:4)?

We desperately need the answer. Our own lives leave a trail of unfinished tasks. Unanswered letters, unvisited friends, unwritten articles and unread books haunt the quiet moments when we stop to evaluate. A mother's work is never finished, and neither is that of a student, teacher, minister or any Christian I know. Even a man's home is no longer his castle since radio, television and telephone have breached the walls with their endless distractions.

Will we escape in five years? No, because children will come and require our time. Greater experience in our job and church brings more exacting assignments. We find ourselves working more and enjoying it less.

But it isn't hard work that hurts us. We all know what it is to go full speed for long hours, totally involved in an important task. The resulting weariness is matched by a sense of achievement and joy. Not hard work, but doubt and indecision produce anxiety as we review a month and feel oppressed by the pile of unfinished tasks. Gradually, we sense uneasily that we may have failed to do the important. We have been driven by the winds of other people's demands onto a reef of frustration.

Several years ago a man with years of executive experience said to me. "Your greatest danger is letting the urgent things crowd out the important." The problem is that the important thing rarely has to be done today, or even this week. Those extra hours of prayer and Bible study, that non-Christian friend to be visited, the book that requires careful study: These projects do not have to be done today. The urgent tasks are the ones that call for instant action. They seem at the moment to be important and irresistible, so they devour our energy. But in the light of time's perspective their importance fades, and we see the important things we have failed to do. We've been slaves to the tyranny of the urgent.

CHRIST'S EXAMPLE ESCAPE

Is there escape from this pattern? The answer lies in the life of our Lord. On that last night, with many useful tasks undone and urgent human needs unmet, He still had the peace of knowing He had finished God's work.

The gospel records show that Jesus worked hard. After describing a busy day Mark writes, "That evening, at sundown, they brought to him all who were sick or possessed with demons. And the whole city was gathered together about the door. And he healed many who were sick with various diseases, and cast out many demons" (1:32-34).

On another occasion the demand of the ill and maimed caused Him to miss supper and work so late that His disciples thought He was beside Himself (Mark 3:21). One day after a strenuous teaching session Jesus and His disciples went out in a boat, and even a storm didn't waken Him (Matthew 4:37, 38). What a picture of exhaustion.

Yet His life was never feverish; He had time for people. He could spend hours talking to one person, such as the Samaritan woman at the well. His life showed a wonderful balance, a sense of timing. When His brothers wanted Him to go to Judea, He replied, "My time has not come" (John 7:6). Jesus did not ruin His gifts by haste.

Immediately following the above account of Jesus' busy day, we read that ". . . in the morning, a great while before day, He rose and went out to a lonely place, and there He prayed" (Mark 1:35). Here is the secret of Jesus' life and work for God: *He prayerfully waited for His Father's instructions,* and for the strength to follow them. He had no God-given finely-drawn blueprint, but the Father's will day by day in a life of prayer. And so He warded off the urgent in the interest of the important.

Lazarus' death illustrates this. What could have been more important than the urgent message from Mary and Martha, "Lord, he whom You love is ill" (John 11:3)? John records the Lord's response in these paradoxical words: "Now Jesus loved Martha and her sister and Lazarus. So when He heard that he was ill, He stayed two days longer in the place where He was" (vs. 5, 6). What was the urgent need? Obviously to prevent the death of this beloved brother. But the important thing from God's point of view was to raise Lazarus from the dead. This Jesus did as the sign of His magnificent claim, "I am the resurrection and the life; he who believes in me though he die, yet shall he live" (v. 25).

We may wonder why our Lord's ministry was so short, why it could not have lasted another five or ten years, why so many wretched sufferers were left in their misery. Scripture gives no answer to these questions, and we leave them in the mystery of God's purposes. But we do know that Jesus' prayerful waiting for God's instructions freed Him from the tyranny of the urgent. It gave Him a sense of direction, set a steady pace, enabled Him to do every task *God* assigned. And on the last night He could say, "I have finished the work which thou gavest me to do."

ESCAPE

Freedom from the tyranny of the urgent appears in the example and promise of our Lord. At the end of a vigorous debate with the Pharisees in Jerusalem, Jesus said to those who believed in Him: "If you continue in my word, you are truly my disciples, and you will know the truth, and the truth will make you free. . . . Truly, truly, I say to you, everyone who commits sin is a slave to sin. . . . So if the Son makes you free, you will be free indeed" (John 8:31, 32, 34, 36).

Many of us have experienced Christ's deliverance from the penalty of sin, but are we letting Him free us from the tyranny of the urgent? He points the way: "If you *continue* in my word." This is the way to freedom. Through prayerful meditation on God's Word we gain His perspective.

P. T. Forsyth once said, "The worst sin is prayerlessness," because when we fail to pray we're saying that we don't need God's guidance and strength. The opposite of such independence is prayer in which we acknowledge our dependence upon God.

Prayerful waiting on God is indispensable to effective service. It is a time to catch our breath and fix new strategy. In this daily fellowship, the Lord frees us from the tyranny of the urgent. He shows us the truth about Himself, life, ourselves, our tasks. He impresses on our minds those we should undertake. The need itself is not the call; the call must come from God, and He knows our limitations. "The Lord pities those who fear him. For he knows our frame; he remembers that we are dust" (Psalm 103:13, 14). It is not God who loads us until we bend or crack with a nervous breakdown, heart attack, ulcer or stroke. These come from our own inner compulsions coupled with the pressure of circumstances.

This principle of taking time out for evaluation is recognized by the modern business man. When Greenwalt was president of DuPont, he said, "One minute spent in planning saves three or four minutes in execution." Many a salesman has revolutionized his business and multiplied his profits by setting aside Friday afternoon to plan carefully the major activities for the coming week. If an executive is too busy to stop and plan, he may find himself replaced by another man who does. If the Christian is too busy to stop, take spiritual inventory, and receive his assignments from God, he becomes a slave to the tyranny of the urgent. He may work day and night to achieve much that seems important to himself and others, but he will not finish the work *God* has for him to do.

A quiet time of meditation and prayer at the start of a day refocuses our relationship with God. It brings recommitment to His will as we think of the hours that lie ahead. In these quiet moments I usually list in order of priority the tasks to be done, taking into account commitments already made. A competent general always draws up his battle plans before he engages the enemy; he does not postpone basic decisions until the firing starts. But he is also prepared to change his plans if an emergency demands it. So I am open to any emergency interruption or unexpected person who may call. Otherwise I try to implement the plans I have already made, before the day's battle against the clock begins.

I have also found it necessary to resist the temptation to accept an engagement when the invitation first comes over the telephone. No matter how clear the calendar may look at the moment, I usually ask for time to pray about it and give an answer in a day or two. Surprisingly the engagement often appears less important once the pleading voice has died out. If I can withstand the urgency of the initial moment, and the event seems important two days later when I have counted the cost, it is more likely to be the will of God.

In addition to my daily quiet time, I try to set aside one hour a week for spiritual inventory. Using a pen, I evaluate the past, record anything God may be teaching me, and plan objectives for the future. I also struggle to set aside most of one day each month for a similar inventory on a longer range. Often I fail. Ironically, the busier we get the more we need this time out but the less able we seem to take it. Like the fanatic, when unsure of our direction we double our speed. And our frantic service for God can even become an escape from God. But when I do succeed, this prayerful thought provides fresh perspective on my work.

Over the years the greatest continuing struggle in my Christian life has been to make adequate time for daily waiting on God, weekly inventory and monthly planning. Since it is so important, Satan will do everything he can to squeeze it out. Yet I know from experience that this is the only way I can escape the tyranny of the urgent. This is how my Lord succeeded. He didn't finish all the urgent tasks in Palestine or all the things He would have liked to do, but He finished "the work which *thou* hast given to me to do." The only alternative to frustration is to be sure that we are doing what God wants. There is no substitute for knowing that this day, this hour, in this place I am doing the will of my Father. Then and only then can I think of all the other unfinished tasks with equanimity and leave them with God.

Some time ago, Simba bullets killed a young man, Dr. Paul Carlson; yet in the providence of God his life's work was finished. Most of us will live longer and die more quietly, but when the end comes, what could give us greater joy than being sure that we have finished the work *God* gave us to do? This is possible by the grace of our Lord Jesus Christ. He has promised deliverance from sin, including the kind of service for God that is dependent on God's direction and power. The way is clear. If we continue in His Word, we are truly His disciples, and He will free us from the tyranny of the urgent, free us to do the important, which is the will of God.*

HIS Magazine, February, 1966, pp. 1-3
Reprinted by permission from HIS, student magazine of Inter-Varsity Christian Fellowship © 1966.

Bibliography

A. CHRISTIAN APOLOGETICS

**1. *Mere Christianity* by C. S. Lewis, Fontana Books.
A very readable introduction to the facts of Christianity.
**2. *Basic Christianity* by John Stott; Inter-Varsity Press.
A precisely written, fact-filled book which focuses on the historical reasons why we believe Christianity to be true and the personal implications of these facts.
  3. *Why Believe?* By Rendle Short; Inter-Varsity Press.
  4. *The Evidence for the Resurrection* by J. N. D. Anderson; Inter-Varsity Press Booklet.

B. THE TIME PROBLEM

 *1. *Have Time and Be Free* by Theodor Bovet; S.P.C.K.
A Swiss psychiatrist speaks of how he seeks to know God's mind in coping with all the demands on his time.
  2. *Managing Your Time* by Ted Engstrom and Alec Mackenzie; Zondervan Publishing House.
Two top Christian executives speak in a very practical way about how to cope with demands on our time.

C. BIBLE STUDY

  1. *A Christian's Guide to Bible Study* by A. Morgan Derham; Hodder and Stoughton.
One of the best introductions to serious Bible study available.
  2. *The New Bible Commentary* and *The New Bible Dictionary;* Inter-Varsity Press.
Two splendid reference books which are "musts" for serious Bible study.
  3. *The Daily Study Bible* by William Barclay; St. Andrews Press.
A 17 volume set of paper-back commentaries on the

New Testament noted for the interesting background they give to each passage. The author has the knack of distilling complex scholarly knowledge into simple, accurate statements.

4. Scripture Union Bible Notes.
Various quarterly booklets geared to different age groups designed for daily Bible study.

5. *Christian Maturity* by E. Stanley Jones; Hodder and Stoughton.
One of a series of excellent daily devotional guides by one of the outstanding Christian leaders of today.

D. PRAYER

**1. *Prayer; Conversing With God* by Rosalind Rinker; Zondervan Publishing House.

*2. *A Diary of Private Prayer* by John Baillie, Oxford Press.
A prayer for each morning and evening with the opposite page left blank for your own prayer requests.

E. EVANGELISM AND SOCIAL ACTION

1. *Into the World* by J. N. P. Anderson; Falcon Books.

2. *The Social Conscience of the Evangelical* by Sherwood Wirt; Scripture Union.

*3. *Christianity and the Social Order* by Archbishop William Temple; S.C.M. Press.
Now a classic.

4. *The Christian Persuader.*
Chapter 10 is entitled "Is Evangelism Relevant?"

F. PROBLEMS IN EVANGELISM

1. *Our Guilty Silence* by John R. Stott; Hodder and Stoughton.

2. *Cooperative Evangelism* by Robert O. Ferm; Zondervan.

Chapter 3

The Practice of Witness

The Practice of Witness

Group Exercises

PHASE I: *The Lecture — Part I* (10 minutes)

Answer the questions below as you listen to the tape:

1. Where is our prime responsibility for witness?

2. Why?

3. What is the essence of verbal witness?

4. What is a Christian conversationalist?

5. Why are small-groups so valuable as a means of witness?

PHASE II: *Sharing* (30 minutes)

"What does it mean, in concrete terms, to be honest as a Christian?" This is the question we want now to probe. Below are three situations. For each, write how you as a Christian would react in all honesty. Take five minutes to answer these. The rest of the time will then be used for discussion with the whole group.

1. You are having a cup of coffee with a friend. The friend says: "You seem to be pretty involved in this discussion group of yours. What is it all about?" You answer:

2. You have just finished the eighteenth hole of golf. As you walk back to the club house, your partner wipes the sweat off his brow, replaces his hat, and says: "One thing I don't understand about you is why you still go to church. What do you get out of it?" You answer:

3. You discover one day, that a young father in your neighborhood with three small children is out of work and that the family is struggling. You *act,* as a Christian, by:

PHASE III: *The Art of Listening* (15 minutes)

First of all, the leader and a volunteer will demonstrate this exercise. Then you will break up into two's, and will spend five minutes discussing the subject: "The Church as an institution has outlived its usefulness." One person will represent the "Yes" side while the position of the other person will be "No, this is not so." (Do not worry if the side you take does not necessarily express your own viewpoint.)

PHASE IV: *The Lecture — Part II* (3 minutes)

As you listen to the explanation of the problem-solving exercise list the four aims of a person involved in a helping situation. Note these carefully as they will serve as the basis for the next exercise.

1.

2.

3.

4.

PHASE V: *Problem Solving* (30 minutes)

Divide into groups of three. Each person must now choose a problem in which he would like help.

It should be a significant problem in which the individual is involved and which he would like to see changed. It should be something that involves relationships with other people, either individuals or organizations. For example: "I am a Sunday school teacher and I am having trouble in keeping the children's attention during the lesson."

A. *First Run:* After having been given a few minutes to decide on the problem, the exercise begins with No. 1 trying to help No. 2 with his problem (which No. 2 will state) while No. 3 acts as an observer. After five minutes the exercise will be stopped and there will be three minutes for discussion. The observer (No. 3) first gives his evaluation, then the consultant (No. 1) says how far he felt he made progress and the consultee (No. 2) says how he felt. Then general discussion follows (within the triads) *not* about details of the problem involved but about the effectiveness of the consultation.

The observer should note points like: Did the helper monopolize the conversation or not? Was he a good listener? Was he judgmental? Did he give too much advice? Did he argue for his own point of view? Did he help the other to see the issues better or, if they got that far, come to a decision about the next step?

B. *Second Run*: The procedure is repeated with No. 2 helping No. 3 with the problem and No. 1 observing.

C. *Third Run*: As above with No. 3 helping No. 1 and No. 2 observing.
   Feedback: The whole group will then discuss what they felt about the exercise and what they learned.

As we try to help others in this way, we of course help ourselves and increase our usefulness to the Church. Consultation gets us involved with other people and concerned with the practical application of the principles of Christianity to real life conditions. We learn what "bearing one another's burdens" means. Concern for others and their needs is a key part of Christian love. In consultation we lay our experience and love, in humility, alongside another life in a "shared search."[1]

The Practice of Witness

Study Schedule

READ:

1. *The Text of the Lecture,* assessing constantly your own conversation with your friends, and how you might be able to share Christ with them.
2. *The Supplementary Paper,* "Witnessing Is Not Brainwashing," by Dr. John White, a Canadian psychiatrist, asking yourself what the statement, "to witness is to be honest" means.
3. *Sections from those books in the Bibliography* which deal with aspects of the lecture which especially puzzle or interest you.

CONSIDER FOR YOURSELF:

"Sharing Our Faith," a Bible study taken from Mark 5.

ACT:

1. *By drawing up a list* of your friends, relatives, associates and neighbors with whom you could speak about Christianity.
2. *By praying* for these people.
3. *By speaking,* this week, to at least one person about Christianity.

Beginning to Be a Witness

". . . our task as laymen is to live our personal communion with Christ with such intensity as to make it contagious."[2]

Paul Tournier

We have now come to the point at which we must think about translating our ideas into action. We may be thoroughly convinced that it is the responsibility of each Christian to be a witness (and hence *our* responsibility). We may have become aware of what it is that has hindered our own witness in the past. Now we must consider what is involved in turning these ideas about witness into acts of outreach.

It is incredibly difficult, however, for some of us to do this. I suppose that part of the reason is simply that any new thing is difficult at the beginning. And if our faith has always been a passive, safe sort of affair that demanded little from us except participation in church activities, then to start turning that into an active, outgoing experience is fairly frightening — even though we may know that for us to try to cling to our passivity means that gradually our "faith" will grow cold and meaningless.

INDIVIDUAL WITNESS

How then do we begin? Do we, as one man I read about in England, jump into our car and drive around looking for a person who wants a lift, and then once he is in the car, "thump him with the Gospel"? (his own words). To begin to witness, do we start with the nearest stranger?

Surely not. The first thing we must do is to realize that *our primary responsibility for witness is among our own circle of friends, associates, neighbors and relatives.* God has given each of us a unique sphere of influence. It is here that our witness must focus primarily.

When you think about it, this makes good sense. Seldom is "witness" a one time affair, in which we meet a person, tell him about Christ, and see him become a Christian, then and there. More often, witness is an ongoing process, involving various factors over a period of time. For example, our witness to a friend may involve such things as our reactions to situations, our discussion at various times of different aspects of Christianity, books which we loan our friend, our openness as to what Christ is doing in our life, our acts of service, etc. All these contribute to our friend's growing appreciation of what Christianity is. Slowly our friend comes to understand who Jesus is, and slowly he opens his life to Him, until finally he is ready to take that decisive step in which he gives himself to Christ and asks Him to become his Lord.

This is why our prime responsibility to witness is among those with whom we have natural and continuous contact. Yet I realize that for many Christians it is precisely among their friends and relatives that they seem to have the *least* opportunity to mention their faith. Why is this?

The problem here is two-fold. First, when you think about it, you will realize that with our friends we often, almost unconsciously, seem to *avoid* any situation in which the subject of our faith could be raised. I was once speaking to a group and I was emphasizing the fact that to witness meant simply to be transparently honest before our friends. A girl came up afterward and said: "I think I know what you mean. This evening, as I was leaving for this Bible study, my neighbor asked me where I was going. I said, 'Oh, I'm going to a friend's house.' Now this was true, but I have a feeling that we would have got into a really interesting conversation if I had been fully honest and said, 'Oh, to a friend's house *where we have a weekly Bible study.*' But I was a bit afraid he might want to talk about the Bible study!" When we are honest I think we all have to admit that we have been guilty of avoiding certain situations in which we might be asked to discuss our faith.

As has been said:

> Witnessing is being honest, that is, being true to what God has made you in your speech and in your day-by-day be-

haviour. Such honesty will demand that you talk about Christ to unbelievers with whom you converse. The fact that you have in the past had to create openings to talk about spiritual things proves that subconsciously you have been avoiding the openings that are continually being presented to you . . . If you are even partially honest (total honesty is rare and difficult) in a conversation with an unbeliever, you will find it extremely difficult to avoid talking about Christian things. *Do you say it is difficult to witness? I maintain that with a little honesty, it is almost impossible not to witness.*[3]

The second reason why we seem to have so few opportunities to share our faith with our friends follows on from this. Because we have a tendency to avoid talking about Christ, many of us have grown *insensitive* to the many natural opportunities we have all the time. Think for a moment about the possible situations in which you could quite naturally share about Christ.

1. *Witness by Our Discussion*

Perhaps the most common opportunity arises *when friends discuss their problems with us.* All of us talk with friends constantly about the difficulties, both major and minor, that we are facing. At such points, it is quite natural to share how, as Christians, we face our own problems in the power of Christ.

Consider for example two housewives chatting over tea. One of them comments about the husband of a mutual friend: "What a vile temper that man has. I don't know how she puts up with it. Did you hear what he did when . . . ?" It would be both natural and appropriate in such a situation to say as a Christian (if it were true): "Yes, I really sympathize with the poor man because I've got the same sort of temper — though I must say in the past year since I've been praying regularly about this, I've begun to learn how to cope. . . ." Such openness cannot help but create openness on the other person's part.

Situations in which it is natural to discuss Christ arise constantly in our daily conversations — if only we will become sensitive to them. There is, however, only one way our sensitivity can grow — by, in fact, bringing our Christian experience into our conversation. As we do so, we will become what one man has called, "a Christian conversationalist." To become such ought to be our aim.

As has been written:

> To have dialogue with a gifted Christian conversationalist is a rare and wonderful experience. I will always be thankful for a conversation I had with such a person. He listened to me. He was interested in my struggles, doubts, and hopes. He seemed to understand me. He shared some of the concerns of his own life which were very much like my own. From time to time he asked questions. Finally he prayed with me, not in a condescending way but as a fellow seeker trying to discover God's best. I came away from that conversation a different person.
>
> I am convinced that God intends all Christians to be effective conversationalists. Perhaps this is the highest expression of "the priesthood of all believers." People are eager for love and acceptance. Through the art of conversation we can demonstrate that God knows them, loves them, and understands them.[4]

2. *Witness by Our Actions*

We also have a natural opportunity to witness when we are able *to help out others who are in need.* (Do not forget that as we defined "witness" in chapter one, it involves not just our words, but our *actions* as well.)

This is well illustrated by the experience of a church in Los Angeles which has developed a program whereby the lay people try consciously to help their neighbors in concrete ways when unexpected problems arise. For example, one couple in the church began to get to know a new couple in the neighborhood. This new couple was expecting their third child. When it came to the time for the baby to be born, the women of the church arranged to look after the other children while the mother was in the hospital. They also saw to it that the husband had a proper meal in the evening. When the wife returned home from the hospital, she found awaiting her a gift for the baby as well as a hot casserole for the evening meal.

Soon after this, the couple, who had never had much to do with any church, invited their Christian neighbors over for the evening, mainly to inquire: "Why did you people do this? We aren't members of your church, we are strangers in this neighborhood; yet everyone has been so kind." The Christian neighbors began to explain about their experience of Christ and how He had freed them in a new way to care for others, for no other reason than other people needed help. It was not long after this that the other couple discovered for themselves the reality of Jesus Christ. But it all began because of baby sitting and hot meals!

Such "acts of service" are acts of witness, in that they reflect the love of Christ, and as such, witness in and of themselves. They need not be linked directly with our words. Yet it is interesting to note in how many instances our actions cause questions to be asked of us, giving us a natural opportunity to talk about Christ. This is our aim, of course, because in our explanation we can point to the Christ who is motivating us — and it is He we want others to discover.

I hope it is becoming clear that to witness we do not have to create artificial opportunities. All we have to do is to act and talk like Christians in the numerous situations that already exist — in our home, in our play, and in our work. The Communists have discovered this fact. Observes Douglas Hyde:

> For (the Communists), their place of work provides them with an ideal opportunity of doing a job for Communism. The Communist sees it like this: it is in the nature of the capitalist society to bring increasingly large numbers of people into daily contact with each other in order to produce the goods, and therefore the profits which the capitalist employers demand. This is one of the means by which the capitalist class digs its own grave — it cannot escape from

doing so, no matter how it may try. For, by bringing together ever-larger numbers of workpeople into ever-larger factories, the capitalist class presents the Communists in them with a ready-made audience. From the Communist's point of view, they are by the nature of things obliged to provide him with a golden opportunity for disseminating his ideas amongst large numbers of workpeople.

You may announce and organise a public meeting and if you work sufficiently hard, perhaps for weeks and months on end and, if you have a good or well-known speaker, you may be able to get together an audience of 5,000 people. If you do, you will probably consider that you have had more than usual success. But capitalist society presents the Communist with, maybe, scores of thousands of people as a ready-made audience, not just once, but every day. This audience is presented to him free, at the enemy's expense. The capitalists provide the building, they get the people together and give him the opportunity to be with them for six, seven, maybe eight or more hours a day. He stands amongst them at his machine as they work, he eats with them in the canteen at lunchtime, chats with them during the morning and afternoon tea breaks.

The most important part of the Communist's day is, or should be, that which he spends at work. He sees his work as giving him a wonderful opportunity to do a job for the cause. By way of contrast, the average Christian feels that his time for going into action on behalf of his beliefs begins after he has returned from his day's work, had a meal, changed and has just an hour or two left — when he is already tired — to give to his cause.[5]

GROUP WITNESS

Thus far it may have sounded as if witness is exclusively an individual affair. While it is true that as individuals we have a responsibility of love to be open to our friends about the power of Jesus Christ, it is also true that frequently the most effective witness springs from the *community* of believers. In fact, I am personally more and more convinced that in this day and age, some of the deepest and most significant witness occurs when a small group of Christians and non-Christians meet together to discuss Christianity.

For example, a few years ago a friend of mine became concerned about his circle of friends. He had spoken on many occasions with these friends, all of them business and professional people, about various aspects of Christianity. They were interested in varying degrees. Yet none of them really seemed to have come to grips with the reality of Jesus Christ. Christianity was only of academic interest to them.

He decided, after long thought and prayer, to invite these friends to come together at his home, once a week, for eight weeks. He proposed that during this time they discuss together John Stott's book, *Basic Christianity,* in which there is a superb presentation of Jesus Christ and the personal implications of His life, death and resurrection.

The reactions of his friends to this invitation varied from real delight to outright fear! But, with only a few exceptions, they all came. And they continued coming week by week, drawn by the vitality of Jesus Christ whom they were investigating and by the sheer fun of being together with other like-minded people. By the end of the series several had decided to follow Christ. Others who had been dormant Christians for years, re-discovered a vitality of faith.

I could repeat scores of similar stories. For example, Dr. Sam Shoemaker, the late rector of Calvary Episcopal Church in Pittsburgh, Pennsylvania and a pioneer in using small groups, tells the story of a 28-year-old salesman whom he met one day at his church. This man had just "dropped in" at the nearest Episcopal Church his first Sunday in Pittsburgh, having been sent there by his company to begin a new job. Dr. Shoemaker invited him to join a group of businessmen who met weekly at lunch time for the purpose of discovering together ways to make Christianity meaningful at their job. For some reason this newcomer accepted the invitation.

The young man was intrigued by what he found at the group. He had never before been in anything like it. The meetings soon became relevant to him personally. In his new

97

job he found himself unexpectedly in charge of people much older than himself and he was finding it difficult to cope. So he started trying to do what the other young businessmen in the group were doing, namely, putting his problems before Christ. He was amazed at how prayer helped. Instead of lying awake at night agonizing over the decisions he must make, he was able to sleep and leave home each day with a clear and open mind.

But gradually, he began to realize that, "I was sort of using God for my own ends, and coming to the conclusion that it was about time I began repaying something of what I received." In conversation with Dr. Shoemaker after one of the meetings he decided, in a rather half-hearted way, to commit his life to Christ. As he put it: "There weren't any brilliant flashes of light nor any miracles which would seem to change my life — not yet there weren't!"

Despite this initial hesitancy and doubt, he kept on praying and going to the group meetings and trying to follow Christ. He gradually found that his new faith was beginning to solve problems for him personally. Being naturally gregarious, he started telling his secretary and co-workers what was happening. Today this man is well-known as an individual who is able, in quite a remarkable way, to live by Christian principles in his business. He is a man actively following Christ.[6]

Such stories are becoming increasingly common — stories of men and women, on the fringe of Christianity or completely "anti-Church," drawn into a small group in which they have the opportunity to consider for themselves the claims of Christ; and then finding, to their amazement, that they are drawn into deep commitment to Christ.[7]

Why is this so? What is there about a small group that makes it such a splendid means of witness? For one thing, a group provides the *ongoing exposure to Christianity* so vital to spiritual discovery. As Sam Shoemaker put it: "Before the average person comes into a vital Christian experience, he usually needs a period of exposure to the experience of others."[8]

Secondly, a group is a *natural way* of exposing people to Christianity. Groups are familiar to all of us, since we spend hours daily in informal groups of various kinds discussing everything under the sun. The same cannot be said of the lecture (or sermon) format. Not only does our familiarity with groups make them natural, but so does the fact that groups generally meet in a familiar place — a home, an office, etc. Consider for a moment which would be easier; to get a neighbor to come with you to a special series of meetings at your church, or to get him to come into your home for a meal with several other couples, followed by a discussion. In the former situation he would have to come into an unfamiliar building, mix with a group of largely unknown people and participate in a meeting in which he would not fully understand what was expected of him (e.g. "Do I stand or kneel now?").

Thirdly, small groups are of such value because they provide the opportunity for *face-to-face interaction*. So often we are asked to consider Christianity without any chance to interact with the presentation. Yet we need to do this if we are to understand how Christ can meet us in all our uniqueness, with all of our particular needs.

Fourthly, in the small group there is not (or should not be) any *artificial pressure* placed upon a person to accept other people's points of view. The aim of the group is not to bludgeon a person into the Kingdom of God, but merely to provide for him the basic facts of the Gospel, in an atmosphere of love, acceptance and discussion. Furthermore, these "facts" are presented not as abstract theological doctrines, but as the real experiences of real people. In such an atmosphere a person is irresistibly drawn to Christ by the sheer power of His magnificent presence.

Fifthly, perhaps the major reason why small groups work is that they meet a fundamental, deep-seated need within each of us, namely the need for fellowship. We all recognize that to live we need food, air, and sleep. But we often forget that just as vital to life (full life that is) is *fellowship,* i.e. deep, meaningful contact with other people. That this is so can easily be seen in the fact that there are few full-time hermits in the world today!

Paul Tournier, a Swiss psychiatrist, tells of a young woman he counseled:

> She lived in one of those great modern buildings, with countless one-room flats, where the neighbours' noises come from every floor. She knew none of those neighbours with whom she rubbed shoulders in the elevator daily, and they did not know her. She had no intimate friends. Her room was even in the same building where she worked. She rarely went out for any reason except for the odd hurried shopping trip. Before falling asleep she would switch on the radio, ". . . and so, we bid you a very pleasant good night!" It was a human voice, speaking to *her*.[9]

We need one another. And yet we seem so cut-off, despite our countless acquaintances. Part of this is due to the barriers we all erect around ourselves to keep others away from the "real us." Yet we crave the opportunity to drop our mask a little, expose our "true self" and find that we are still loved and accepted.

This can happen in a Christian fellowship group. This is, in fact, the nature of an authentic Christian group — a body of people who have faced the dark sides of their nature, found forgiveness in Christ and from one another, and are able therefore to live transparently honest lives before one another. A non-Christian, entering such a group, finds the experience of such a fellowship virtually irresistible.

Remember what Professor Weber wrote in Chapter One about the early Christians:

> The astonishing Christian community life and the Christian service . . . gave the necessary sounding board for the spoken message to become real proclamation instead of empty declaration. . . . Tertullian wrote the following famous words: "Our care for people who cannot help themselves, our works of charity have become a distinguishing mark by which our enemies recognize us: 'See how these Christians love one another,' they say (for they themselves

hate one another)." . . . Commenting on this ministering community life of the early Christians, A. Harnack exclaimed: ". . . what power of attraction it must have exercised, as soon as its object came to be understood. It *was this, and not any evangelist, which proved to be the most effective missionary.*"[10]

CONCLUSION

We are called, as Christians, to be witnesses first and foremost among our natural (and unique) circle of friends, relatives and acquaintances — the people with whom we come into contact day by day.

On an individual level we have many opportunities to share our faith (if we will become sensitive to these opportunities and open in our relationships). Our personal witness can then be complemented by means of a small group in which our friends will have a chance to discuss Christianity without pressure, in a familiar setting where the rare experience of fellowship is found. That this is so is illustrated not only by the example of the early Church, but by the numerous testimonies in the growing literature about the effect of small groups within the Church. It is because this is so that we invite you to continue in this experiment of outreach by means of groups.

Sharing Our Faith With Others

"Me talk about Christianity — I wish I could but I just can't! What would I say?" How often have *you* felt like this?

You are, of course, not alone in your feeling. Most people avoid sharing their faith with the same fervor that they would avoid sharing the plague. It is strange, is it not, how hard it seems to be to talk about Christ with non-church friends?

Yet, sharing with others the exciting things Christ has done is the norm in the New Testament. For example, there is a story recorded in Mark 5:1-20. Perhaps there are some lessons here for us.

> They came to the other side of the sea, to the country of the Gerasenes. And when Jesus had come out of the boat there met him out of the tombs a man with an unclean spirit, who lived among the tombs; and no one could bind him any more, even with a chain; for he had often been bound with fetters and chains, but the chains he had wrenched apart, and the fetters he broke in pieces; and no one had the strength to subdue him. Night and day among the tombs and on the mountains he was always crying out and bruising himself with stones. And when he saw Jesus from afar, he ran and worshipped him; crying out with a loud voice he said, "What have you to do with me, Jesus, Son of the Most High God? I adjure you by God, do not torment me." For he had said to him, "Come out of the man, you unclean spirit!" And Jesus asked him, "What is your name?" He replied, "My name is Legion, for we are many." And he begged him eagerly not to send them out of the country. Now a great herd of swine was feeding on the hillside, and they begged him, "Send us to the swine, let us enter them." So he gave them leave. And the unclean spirits came out, and entered the swine; and the herd, numbering about two thousand, rushed down the steep bank into the sea, and were drowned in the sea.
>
> The herdsmen fled, and told it in the city and in the country. And people came to see what it was that had happened. And they came to Jesus, and saw the demoniac sitting there, clothed and in his right mind, the man who had

had the legion; and they were afraid. And those who had seen it told what had happened to the demoniac and to the swine. And they began to beg Jesus to depart from their neighbourhood. And as he was getting into the boat, the man who had been possessed with demons begged him that he might be with him. But he refused, and said to him, "Go home to your friends, and tell them how much the Lord has done for you, and how he has had mercy on you." And he went away and began to proclaim in the Decapolis how much Jesus had done for him; and all men marveled.

Answer the following questions by reference to the story in Mark 5:

1. *Who* are mentioned in this story?

   (a) _____

   (b) _____

   (c) _____

   (d) _____

   (d) _____

   (e) _____

   (f) _____

   (g) _____

2. *Where* does the incident take place? Using the text and a Bible map try to locate the area.

   _____

3. This story took place at the side of a lake "where there were many caves in the limestone rock, and many of these caves were used as tombs in which bodies were laid. At the best of times, it was an eerie place; as night fell it must have been grim indeed."[11]

4. What title did the man use to address Jesus?

   _____

5. Though men often hesitate in their judgment of who Jesus is, note that the supernatural beings knew exactly who He was.

6. From what you know of Jewish dietary laws, could these herdsmen have been Jews? Why or why not?

   _____

   _____

7. Imagine now that you are a journalist. Here is a good story for you. Write an account of this incident in your own words as if you were doing so for the Palestine Times. Include:
   (a) A vivid description of the man and his history.
   (b) His encounter with Jesus.
   (c) The reaction of the demons, and their end.
   (d) The response of the local population.

8. What was the first reaction of the populace to Jesus? Why do you suppose they reacted to Him as they did?

   _____

   _____

9. What was their second reaction to Him, after He had left?

   _____

   _____

10. What changed their minds? _____

   _____

   _____

11. What does this teach you about the value of sharing with your neighbors what Jesus has done?

   _____

   _____

_____

_____

12. What do you suppose the cured demoniac told his friends about Jesus?

_____

_____

_____

13. What could you tell your friends that Jesus has done for you? Be honest and be natural in answering. Spend time on this.

_____

_____

_____

_____

_____

_____

Try now to share this with someone.

14. Every venture has a beginning. So too with sharing our faith. Our initial attempts may well sound unnatural and strained, but they are beginnings and quite necessary. _Today_ is the day to start sharing, not tomorrow. Try to be conscious today of wanting to share your faith. Sharing the truth of Christ with a friend is an act of love. This is part of what it means to love others.*

_____

*Adapted from: _Learning to Love People_ by Richard Peace (Grand Rapids: Zondervan Publishing House, 1968) pp. 24-30.

Action

As one of the first steps in becoming a witness, we ought to give some thought to who the people are with whom we have natural contact. So this week:

1. *Make a list* of the people with whom you could share your faith. Think about your neighbors, the people at the club, friends, colleagues, relatives, etc. Do this prayerfully. Let God direct your thinking.

   1.   4.

   2.   5.

   3.   6.

2. *Pray* for these people. Pray for their needs. Pray that you will have the chance to speak to at least one of these people this week about Christianity.

3. *Be sensitive,* this week, to natural opportunities to discuss Christianity. Try to talk with at least one of the people on your list. You need not say much. Just the odd word here or there is sufficient. Do not think you are expected to deliver a polished, theological statement on the nature of Christianity! Just be sensitive and be honest.

   During the next group session you will have the chance to discuss your experience of trying to share with others.

Witnessing Is Not Brainwashing

By John White

Why are there abortive conversions? Is it our fault or the devil's?

I first hit evangelistic brainwashing in England in 1945. I had been assigned to help a girl who had "gone forward" the previous night, and who had waked up the next morning to realize that she had been tricked into a decision. Her distress and confusion disturbed me profoundly.

You might argue that her conversion was genuine, and that her subsequent reaction was of the devil. I remember taking that line at the time. Now I am much more inclined to feel that her conversion was psychological, but not spiritual.

Let me define my terms.

In one sense all conversion is psychological. Every conversion includes decision and a change of outlook; and decision and changed outlook are psychological phenomena. But while in spiritual conversion the emotional changes are the result of God's working, in a purely psychological conversion they result from a technique or from emotional pressure. They do not represent a miracle of grace.

The distinction began to dawn on me when I heard of the "evangelistic" techniques used by Chinese Communists just after the revolution. They held rallies complete with Communist choruses, testimonies, "dynamic" speakers, appeals and personal workers. The devil's counterfeit? Not exactly. Rather it was the Chinese way of using, openly and deliberately, techniques which some evangelists (perhaps unconsciously) use to get converts.

Our minds are subject to certain laws, and to a limited degree they are open to manipulation. If in a large crowd you make me laugh, then cry, then laugh, then cry again, and if in addition you repeat certain phrases insistently, and alternately berate and comfort me, my mind will become increasingly like putty in your hands if I am not on my guard.

There may come a point at which you can do what you like with me. My judgment is impaired, my conscience is inflamed, my emotions make everything seem different. If in such a condition I make the decision you want me to make, whatever that "decision" may be, I will probably experience relief, joy and peace. This is a well-known psychological phenomenon. The techniques for demonstrating it are equally well-known. Even if I am on my guard they may be hard to resist.

But true spiritual conversion is something vastly more profound. It has a non-material, non-psychological dimension. It yields more than temporary joy and peace. It gives rise to meekness, a hunger and thirst for righteousness, poverty of spirit, and all the fruits of righteousness.

If you ever present the Gospel in a public meeting, you must know what you are doing. Be on your guard against using your preaching skills to perform mass psychotherapy. Remember that you are to be collaborating with the Holy Spirit, so do not be so intent on getting big numbers of conversions that you take over His job. Your job is to explain God's Word, and to point out how it applies; His work is to make the Word so stick in a man's conscience that he suffers conviction. Therefore, don't play on a man's conscience by telling awesome stories. Let the Holy Spirit do the convicting and the awakening of fear. Stories are to illustrate obscure points, not to give your congregation the creeps.

Does this mean that all evangelistic techniques are wrong?

No, I do not think so. It is impossible to do anything without some kind of technique. We need technique to communicate truth clearly. But techniques become immoral when either consciously or unconsciously we use them to tamper with another man's will, emotions or conscience. They also become immoral when they assume more importance in our thinking than the Spirit of God. They become immoral when results matter more to us than people do.

FALSE EMOTION

I am not against emotion in preaching, but I am against emotionalism. I am not against earnest persuasion, but I am against using tricks to make a man change his mind. Paul pleaded with men and women, weeping as he pleaded. This is magnificent. The Gospel of Jesus Christ is not a cold intellectual proposition, any more than the plight of a Christless man is a matter of mere academic interest.

The danger of psychological manipulation does not confine itself to mass rallies, however. Techniques of personal evangelism can be just as dangerous.

Ever come across people who listen to you explain the Gospel and then say: "Oh, I've been through that already"? You question them and find that they "accepted the Lord" when some over-zealous personal worker pushed too hard. It is true that some such "converts" may represent regenerate men and women who are backsliding. But I am equally certain that many more are the result of evangelistic brainwashing by "personal workers."

Part of our trouble arises from our desperation for results. "Full-time" workers have to prove they are laborers worthy of their hire. They have to get results and are as desperate to do so as salesmen. Christian students prove their Christian manhood (like braves prove their physical manhood) by taking a few scalps.

Now, results are admirable. We should be bothered when people around us do not get saved. We should be very bothered. But results have to be genuine to be any good. It is regeneration that fits a man for heaven, not going through the motions of a psychological conversion.

Again, what about the motive I have in wanting results? Does it spring from concern for my neighbor? Does the love of Christ constrain me? Do I yearn for God's glory? Or am I just trying to prove something?

FALSE MOTIVE

Another problem underlying our passion for results is that we belong to a salesman culture. The real representative of the twentieth century is not the scientist or the missile man, but the salesman. He is the man who really keeps the wheels turning.

And the success of a salesman is measured by the number of things he can sell. If he sells things, he is "in."

Many salesmen have secret doubts about the quality of the product they are selling. They must repress these doubts, however, and use the technique in which they have been schooled. Indeed, big companies have their own techniques for keeping the salesman's morale at a high pitch.

The salesman must dress well and drive a nice car. This creates an aura of success, and success breeds success. He must be "interested in" his customers, and his interest must be "genuine." (Yet can any interest be genuine when the ultimate motive is a sale, the commission and the kudos?) The salesman must demonstrate not only the virtue of his products, but that his product is just what the client needs. The Fuller Brush man is trying genuinely to help Mrs. Smith to solve her housekeeping problems, but she must solve them *now*. Why wait? An unparalleled offer is being made to her of something she needs now. She will actually be saving money by buying brushes.

Living in a world of door-to-door salesmen and their more sophisticated cousins, the television and radio commercials, of magazine ads and a thousand and one publicity stunts, it is only natural that we should think of the Gospel as one more thing to sell. Indeed, many teachers openly state that evangelism is a matter of salesmanship.

The comparisons are obvious. We *do* have something the whole world needs. We *are* responsible to get the knowledge of this something (or Someone) to every creature. Time *is* important. Men and women *should* be deciding for our product (excuse the loathesome word).

But there are dangers in the comparison. Mrs. Smith may (under the salesman's technique) buy brushes and later realize that it was not what she wanted to do at all. In a mild way she has been brain-washed. It will be annoying for her, but no great tragedy. It is a far more tragic thing if a man's decision for Christ represents merely giving way to Christian salesmanship.

FALSE HOPE

In the first place, if the Holy Spirit has not been at work in his heart, he is not born again. His "faith" is not saving faith. He has a false hope.

On the other hand if he later reacts against his "conversion," his "sales-resistance" will increase sharply against the Gospel in the future. All over the world there are vast numbers of people who are doubly on their guard against the Gospel because they have passed through a spurious conversion experience.

What is more, the salesman concept is full of moral pitfalls. It goes against the very nature of witness. Dress well? Why? To impress? For testimony's sake? Does testimony consist of a sharp suit and button-down collars? Or are we confusing testimony with reputation and "public image"?

Worse still. Are you one of those miserable Christians who is trying to put on a victorious front "to attract people to Christ"? This of course is the spiritual equivalent of the sharp suit. You smile (or you are supposed to) because a Christian is joyful. You try to be Christ-like though you have no idea of what "Christ-likeness" is.

It is part of the technique. You must attract people to Christ. And if this means suppressing some of the real you and putting on a big act in public, well, that is part of the testimony. The real you pops out at home where there is no one but God to see you. And He doesn't matter, for He is not a customer; He's already on the right side.

Has it never dawned on you that the essence of witness is just plain honesty? You are salt — whether you feel like it or not. You are not told to act like salt, but to be what you are. You are light. God has done a work in your life. Don't try to shine. Let the light that God put there shine out.

BEING HONEST

Now to let your light shine demands no more than honesty. It demands honesty before unbelievers. In fact such honesty is in itself 90 percent of witnessing. Witnessing is not putting on a Christian front so as to convince prospective customers. Witnessing is being honest, that is, being true to what God has made you in your speech and in your day-by-day behavior.

Such honesty will demand that you talk about Christ to unbelievers with whom you converse. The fact that you have in the past had to create openings to talk about spiritual things proves that subconsciously you have been avoiding the openings that are continually being presented to you.

We all hide our real selves behind a front. To preserve the image that we create demands that we talk, laugh, behave in a certain way. Our talk is designed to create an impression on people we talk to, to build up or preserve the image of ourselves we wish to sell. Now for many of us, "witnessing" means adding certain Christian features to this image. But in doing so we are preaching ourselves, not Christ.

On the other hand, real witness means abolishing the front behind which we hide, not modifying it. To live behind a front is to hide my light under a bushel. It is falseness; and falseness is opaque to divine light.

If you are even partially honest (total honesty is rare and difficult) in a conversation with an unbeliever, you will find it extremely difficult to avoid talking about Christian things. Do you say it is difficult to witness? I maintain that with a little honesty, it is almost impossible not to witness.

HONEST IGNORANCE

Now, honesty will also demand admitting that we do not know everything. A good salesman is never stumped for answers. But you are not called to be a salesman, but to be a witness; that is, to be open about what you know and have experienced.

Are you waiting until you have all the answers before you start to witness? Don't. By all means think through answers to problems, but do not postpone witnessing until you have them all. Be prepared to say you don't know. No one will be surprised. God does not depend upon the debating powers of Christians.

Three years ago some Moody Bible Institute students had a meeting in the University of Chicago. During question-time a number of difficult questions were asked, and the Moody students had the good sense to admit they could not answer some of them.

Their honesty was an integral part of their witness.

And it accomplished its purpose. One University of Chicago faculty member publicly expressed interest in hearing more. He said that for the first time he had met Christians who admitted they didn't know everything. This, he said, far from lessening his confidence in them, had actually awakened it.

HONEST EVALUATION

Honesty will also demand the acknowledgment of failure. Failure is bad, but deceit about failure is worse. The end never justifies the means.

I do not mean that honesty means giving way to all your worst instincts. But I do contend that to admit to anger is better than to pretend that you are not angry. I also contend that to admit to failure in your Christian life, far from being prejudicial to testimony, may even be a part of it. Your honesty, of itself, is witness. It takes real spiritual grace and courage to admit failure. Only the man who is not concerned about himself and his public image, but about his Lord, will be able to do it.

But do not sin and failure put Christ to open shame? Yes, indeed they do. But the shame is not removed by covering sin so much as by dealing with it. And clearly you cannot begin to deal with it until you are honest with yourself and, when necessary, with others about it.

Do not wait to witness until you are perfect. Witnessing involves being honest all the time — now. Never cover up your weaknesses to witness. What the world is waiting to see is not a perfect Christian, but the miracle of grace working in a weak, imperfect Christian.

Many Christians today have a tragic misconception of the nature and importance of the role they play in a man's conversion. We should plead with him; not because our pleading saves him, but because we cannot help but plead. We are being true to what the Holy Spirit is doing within us. It is the Holy Spirit who is the real midwife to a new-born soul. To play the Holy Spirit's role is dangerous, immoral and blasphemous.

I believe that in modern evangelism, both public and personal, we are selling our birthright for a mess of pottage. We think we have harnessed the Holy Ghost when all we have harnessed is cheap psychology. We are not presenting a Person but promoting a symbol. We have been called to the glory and honor of being witnesses to the Lord of history and the redeemer of mankind, and we mess about with our silly techniques for "getting decisions."

It is time we quit our blasphemous fooling, and let our light so shine before men that they glorify our Father which is in Heaven.*

---

*Reprinted by permission from *HIS* Magazine (June, 1966, pp. 3-6), student magazine of Inter-Varsity Christian Fellowship. © 1966.

Bibliography

A. PERSONAL GROWTH AND WITNESS

*1. *Dare to Live Now!* by Bruce Larson; Zondervan Publishing House.

Mr. Larson, a Presbyterian Minister, has been involved for some years with *Faith at Work,* an organization which specializes in the development of small groups. All his books reflect a ruthless honesty which leads to a depth of spiritual reality, which is abundantly evident as he writes. You owe it to yourself to read one of Larson's books.

**2. *Setting Men Free* by Bruce Larson; Zondervan Publishing House.

Christ intended us to be "free indeed." How can we realize this goal, living in the twentieth-century world?

*3. *Living on the Growing Edge* by Bruce Larson; Zondervan Publishing House.

The "growing edge" is the point in our life where we are ready and able to learn. This book is all about movement in our Christian life, rather than stagnation. It is about using difficult situations and relationships as a means of growth and not avoiding or denying them because of the threat they are to us.

*4. *The Taste of New Wine* and *A Second Touch* by Keith Miller, Word Books.

The exciting story of one layman's struggle to find reality in his Christian life.

5. *The Miracle of Dialogue* by Reuel Howe, Seabury Press.

6. *The Gospel Blimp* by Joseph Bayly, Zondervan Publishing House.

A most amusing modern-day parable about how *not* to witness in your neighborhood.

B. EXPERIMENTS IN GROUP WITNESS

1. *Groups That Work* by the editors of *Faith at Work,* Zondervan.

2. *Nine Roads to Renewal* by Walden Howard, Word Books.
   Sub-title: A Handbook for Dissatisfied Churches.

3. *Spiritual Renewal Through Personal Groups* by John Casteel, Association Press.

Chapter 4

The Preparation for Witness

Group Exercises

PHASE I: *Group Prayer* (25 minutes)

(The leader will introduce this exercise with some comments on the relationship between witness and prayer.)

A discussion of prayer ought to lead us, quite naturally, to the act of prayer. Hence, this first exercise will involve us in group prayer.

Actually, prayer together is one of the real blessings of a small Christian group. The reason for this is summed up in our Lord's words in Matthew 18:19-20 (Williams translation): "Again, I tell you, if only two of you on earth agree on what you pray for, you will get it from my Father in heaven. For wherever two or three have met as my disciples, I am right there with them." When we pray together, *Jesus is present.* What a staggering fact!

First though, let me reiterate several principles of prayer as a guide for your group:

1. Pray *specifically,* as outlined in the lecture. Not, "Lord, help me to speak more boldly," but "Lord, give me a natural opportunity next week to speak to Carl about You."

2. Pray *simply.* Speak to God as you would to a friend. Share with Him what you are really feeling. There is no need to construct elaborate sentences, filled with lofty theological phrases.

3. Pray *in ordinary English.* There is no special need to use "Thee" and "Thou" in addressing God. This was merely an informal type of speech used in the time of King James, and has no special value, as such, attached to it. (On the other hand, if you are comfortable using such terminology, do not worry about changing your habit.)

4. Pray *briefly.* Long prayers are difficult for others to concentrate on. Long prayers often turn group prayers

into prayer by individuals who happen to be in the same room. Hence today we are going to pray in *single sentences.* A person can then pray more than once.

5. Pray in a *loud enough voice* so that others can hear you easily and thus pray along with you.

Spend the next few minutes thinking about what really concerns you. This is what you want to pray about. For example, think about your experience of trying to discuss Christianity with another person. Jot down some notes. If you have never prayed aloud in a group, you may want to write out your prayer. Remember though — make it only one sentence long!

PHASE II: *The Lecture — Part II* (15 minutes)

As you listen to the lecture, make notes on the five key factors in planning any outreach group.

PHASE III: *Planning an Outreach Evening* (45 minutes)

In the week between Session No. 5 and Session No. 6, you will have the opportunity as a group to conduct an Outreach Evening. This will give you the chance to put into practice a lot of what we have been discussing together.

The aim of this exercise is to plan the details of this Outreach Evening. You will need to make decisions in the five areas outlined in the lecture. For a summary of these areas, as well as suggestions in each, turn to the section at the end of the Text of the Lecture entitled: "Key Factors in Setting Up a Group." The aim now is to be really creative in your planning. To help free you to be creative we will try a new type of group exercise called "Brainstorming." Brainstorming works this way. First, a problem is faced (e.g. what type of meeting will we hold?) Second, the group is asked to make suggestions as quickly as possible without regard to whether the suggestions are practical or not. *All* suggestions will be written on the blackboard. Outlandish ideas are welcomed. *No word of criticism is allowed at this point.* Third, after all suggestions are in, the feasibility of the ideas is discussed and a final decision is reached by the group.

The idea behind brainstorming is that often our creativity is bottled up by the "fear of what others will think." If a non-judgmental situation is set up, really great ideas often emerge. Even foolish suggestions have their place as they often can trigger excellent ideas in the minds of others by means of association.

Industry has latched onto this idea of brainstorming. Executives are locked up in a room for several hours. A problem is presented. Suggestions come fast and furious. The whole proceedings are tape recorded. Later on they are transcribed, and then evaluated at leisure. Superb ideas often result.

Let us begin now. We will not try brainstorming immediately, but will start with a simple discussion about target-groups. Once a decision is made in each area, be sure to appoint someone to put it into effect. Sometimes, final decisions in an area must wait until other areas are discussed.

1. *Target Group*: What sort of individuals will be invited?

2. *Venue*: Where can the Outreach Evening be held? In a home? Whose home? What time? Type of dress?

3. *Type of Group*: Now is the chance to try out brainstorming. What will the target group enjoy? What would be so appealing that your friends could not resist your invitation? Who, now, will look after this area?

4. *Length*: This decision has already been made for you: a single evening.

5. *Content*: Here is the second chance for brainstorming. The leader will explain the material that is available, and you are free to use this, or to add to it, or even to do something totally different. What do you want to communicate? Who will get the equipment necessary?

READ:

1. *The Text of the Lecture,* assessing as you do your relationships with non-church friends.
2. *Sections from those books in the Bibliography* which deal with aspects of the lecture which especially puzzle or interest you.

CONSIDER FOR YOURSELF:

"Prayer Is Conversation With Jesus" in such a way as to discover the reality behind this statement.

ACT:

1. *By inviting friends* to your group's Outreach Evening.
2. *By praying* for these friends.

The Preparation for Witness

Planning Group Outreach

> *"I am obliged to bear witness because I hold, as it were, a particle of light, and to keep it to myself would be the equivalent to extinguishing it."*
>
> Gabriel Marcel

During this past week you made a list of those people with whom it would be natural to discuss Christianity. I hope this was a good experience for you, although I suspect that for some of you this was a rather disturbing exercise — simply because after jotting down one or two names, you found yourself hard put to add any others to the list. Why? Could it perhaps be because you really do not have that much contact with non-Christians — except on a superficial basis? All your real friends are Christians.

OUTREACH TO NON-CHRISTIAN FRIENDS

I recall taking part once in a seminar entitled: "Using the Home for Evangelism." What I remember from this experience is a conversation after the seminar with a middle-aged couple. They said they were quite enthused by what had been said. It all seemed to make such good sense to them. They were willing to use their home as a center for evangelism. "But," they said, "we've racked our brains to think of people to invite over, and we just don't seem to have any friends outside church circles. What do we do? Can *you* perhaps send over some interested non-Christians to our house?" At the time I was rather startled by this — but later on, when others said the same thing, I realized that this was a real problem.

For many, their circle of friends is made up almost exclusively of Christians? Why is this?

There are two factors involved here — one practical and one theological.

On the practical side, it is a simple fact that we make friends at the places where we spend our time. And so, if we devote most of our spare time to church activities, most of our friends will be drawn, quite naturally, from the church. Furthermore, we all feel most comfortable with people who share our viewpoints and hence, as Christians, our real friends tend to be other Christians because we have so much in common with them.

However, we sometimes go one step further and try to justify the fact of our isolation from non-Christians by means of theological reasoning. The argument goes like this: Our Lord Himself told us to be in the world, but not of the world.[1] Hence we must withdraw from all but minimal contact with the "world."

Now is this so? Does this statement by Jesus mean that we are to withdraw into some sort of Christian ghetto? No, otherwise our Lord would never have told us that we were to be the "salt of the earth."[2] Think about salt for a moment and you will see what I mean. Salt is meant to be a flavoring agent. But it cannot do its job of flavoring until it comes into intimate contact with the meat it is supposed to season. Salt is useless if it just sits up on the shelf albeit in a beautiful container.

Now I have a feeling that often our Christian groups are just like that — lots of good "salt" all heaped together in a beautiful building, but largely useless, because the "salt" is not out in the world acting as the flavoring agent.

But then what did Christ mean in telling us not to be of this world? Just this: while we live in the world (we have no choice in this really as it is impossible to eliminate contact with non-Christians) we must not be fooled into accepting the world's understanding of itself. We cannot accept the world's value system, ethos, motivation, etc. We must say to the world: "No, the point of life is not money or pleasure or security. The point of life is to know Christ and hence to live in a loving relationship to God and others while at the same time holding a realistic view of ourselves."

This "closed corporation" mentality, a sort of Christian isolationism, has been a constant barrier to evangelism. Many

123

> Christians have been so afraid of being contaminated by worldliness that they have avoided any social contacts with unconverted persons. As a result, they have no natural bridges for evangelism; what witnessing they do is usually artificial and forced rather than the spontaneous outgrowth of genuine friendship.[3]

After having written all this, let us go back to that list of your friends. If it contains only one or two names, your first job is going to be that of seeking to get to know non-Christians. Actually, when you think about it, numerous opportunities exist already. You undoubtedly live in a neighborhood surrounded by non-church people. You work with non-Christians. Your relatives are probably not all Christians. Make a resolve therefore to try to become "aware" of the non-Christians who do surround you. Then try to get to know them. You will be amazed, I am sure, at what a good response there will be to your friendliness and interest. And who knows where your friendship may lead?[4]

OUTREACH BEGINS WITH PRAYER

Once we have thought about the people with whom it is natural for us to share, the next question is: How then do we begin? In answer to this I would simply say that *witness begins with prayer.*

1. *Specific Prayer*

Think about your list of friends. Your concern for them ought to lead you, quite naturally, to pray for them. But what sort of prayer? "Lord, bless John?" No, *really effective prayer is specific prayer,* that is, prayer that we can really believe God will answer. The trouble with the "blessing" type of prayer is that it is too vague and too general. Furthermore, it is the sort of prayer for which we do not really expect an answer. (How would we ever know, in fact, if God did "bless" John?) As Rosalind Rinker has put it in her book on prayer:

124

We ought to make our prayers faith-sized. A faith-sized request is first of all a request which is just the right "believing" size for your faith. It is not a request which is so large that the very size of it makes you wonder if God will answer. It is a request for a particular situation, in which you pray for a special person or thing, and ask only for that which you can *really believe God will do,* in a given time limit. This does not limit what God can do, but it honestly recognizes the size of your faith. And there is every reason to believe that you will be asking for larger things as your faith grows. . . .

To illustrate faith-sized requests, I'd like to give you the experience of a married couple who moved into a new neighborhood. One of the first requests Mary and Jack made was, "Lord, we'd like to get acquainted with our neighbors, and if they don't know You personally as their Saviour, we'd like to introduce them to You."

That was a fine request and right in line with what God wanted to do. But it was a description of a goal to be reached, not a step to take. They got down to business then, and took the first step.

"Lord," prayed Jack, "I'd like to meet the fellow living next door in some casual way and begin to get acquainted with him. I'd like to begin today, and I believe You can arrange it for me. Thank You, Lord." Mary agreed with Jack in her prayer, and gave thanks with him.

The morning had scarcely turned to afternoon when the answer came. Their children got into a quarrel over a tricycle with the neighbor's children. Both fathers rushed to the scene. Jack took all the blame for his children, and put out his hand. "I'm Jack M., just moved in, glad to meet you." The first request had been answered. The first step had been taken.

The second step: "Lord, I'd like to know what the man is interested in, so we could become friends." The answer came within two days. He was interested in football.

The third step: "Lord, I need two complimentary football tickets, and could I have them by this weekend, please?" The tickets came. The friendship grew.

The fourth step: "Lord, I'd like to invite this new friend

to the Bible class I teach a few miles from here. Would You put it into his heart to accept when I ask him to go with me tonight?" He accepted. All the way over as they drove, they talked about football. All the way home they talked about Jesus Christ, and what it meant for Him to become one of us . . . God become a Man.

The fifth step: "Lord, Mary and I would like to invite my friend and his wife to our home some evening this week and have a little talk and Bible reading together." The friends came, and they read and talked quietly together.

The sixth step: "Lord, next week when I ask them over again, will You prepare their hearts, so that they will be ready to accept You as their Saviour? I believe this is the time to ask for this, and I thank You for all You'll be doing in the meantime to draw them to Yourself." When the next week came, the neighbors willingly and gladly accepted Jesus Christ.[5]

Now it must be admitted that this was an unusual experience. I have seldom found that a relationship develops as easily, or with as immediate and dramatic a response as this one. But nevertheless this is a true illustration of what can happen when we begin to pray faith-sized prayers for our friends.

2. *Prayer and Our Attitudes*

When we engage in such prayer, however, we often find that *the answer to our prayer lies within ourselves.* For example, you may pray: "Lord, I really want to get to know Harry, the chap who sits next to me in the office." As you pray this way, you will begin to become aware of your relationship with Harry. "Why don't I know him better?" you may ask. "After all I have been sitting next to him daily for eight months. I wonder if my attitude to Harry has been the sort which would make it easy for us to become real friends?" The more you think about it, the more you may realize that perhaps you have been a bit judgmental toward him. "I guess I *have* let him know that I disapprove of his long hair and outlandish clothes . . ." and so the inner dialogue goes. If *we really pray for our friends we will come to a new knowledge of our relationship with them.* At times this will involve us in real heart searching, especially if we have been relating in judgment, and not in love. Attitudes speak louder than words and others are quick to sense what we really feel toward them. As Christians we must strive to avoid judgment and to act rather in love.[6] Hence what may begin as a prayer that we may become friends with another person, may be turned into a prayer in which we ask forgiveness for our judgment of that person, and a prayer of request that we may learn how to love him.

3. Prayer as Visualization

As you pray, try to visualize your friends, that is picture them in your mind and then, as you do so, present them in prayer to the Lord.

"Lord, here is John. How I respect that man! What a friend he has been to me. I thank You for his great capacity to care for others. But, Lord, he seems so lost right now. He just doesn't seem to have much purpose or direction in his life any longer. Lord, he needs to know You. . . . How can I help him discover Your reality and power, Lord? Forgive me for being so vague with him about my own relationship to You — even when I knew he was interested. . . ."

And so we pray, presenting our friend and our relationship to God, praying on behalf of our friend and in terms of how God can use us to reach him — trying to see a picture of the difference that could come into his life when Christ has His way with him.

As you do this, you may well find yourself increasingly *praying for one or two friends in particular.* Such special concern may be the Lord saying to you: "Yes, that particular friend is at a unique point in his life where he especially *needs to hear* about me: a point at which he will be *able* to understand who I am." Learn to be sensitive to such leading and quick to act in response.

4. *Prayer and Dependence*

When we pray for others we are acknowledging that for a man to come to an authentic experience of Christ, there must be a work of God the Holy Spirit in his life. Conversion is not merely a psychological phenomenon. To be sure psychological elements are involved in that it is a man and not a stone that is being converted. But the latent potential within each man to turn to God cannot truly be triggered by mere manipulation. If this appears to happen (and it can) this is not true conversion as will be evidenced by the lack of the fruits of the Spirit (i.e. love, joy, peace, etc.) in that man's life. True conversion comes only when a man opens himself to the inner promptings of the Holy Spirit. We must pray for that work of the Holy Spirit in our friend's life.

Furthermore, in prayer we also acknowledge our dependence upon God. We are each called to be ministers for Christ's sake, evangelists, the "salt" of the earth, but this calling is not one which we are able to fulfill in our own power and by means of our own wisdom. We are too imperfect as people. We know too little of God. We see clearly too little of life. We waver and doubt too often. Yet this must not be allowed to discourage us or cause us to withdraw from our calling. God knew what we were like long before He called us to this role — yet He still called *us*. Furthermore, He has not left us alone to fulfill our calling. He is here in the world with us — working through us. In prayer we acknowledge our dependence upon God.

I hope that it is clear by now that the first consideration in planning a small group for outreach is the question of *who*. Who can we invite? The answer is: our uncommitted friends. And then, as we think about these friends, even before we issue an invitation to attend a group, we ought to pray for them.

PLANNING SMALL GROUP OUTREACH

Now we have reached the point where we must move from the question of who, to the question of *how*: *How* do we make small groups work? Last week we discussed *why* groups work. Now we need to know what is involved in planning such groups. Our discussion will revolve around the five basic areas which must be considered before setting up any group.

1. Target Group

The first area we must consider is that of the *target-group*. Who do we want to reach? Are we seeking to reach teenagers or retired people? Are we going to draw together young married couples or is our interest in middle-age parents with teenage children? This is an important question, because experience has taught that it is often difficult to mix a group age-wise. The reason for this is fairly obvious: the interests and needs of the sixteen-year-old schoolgirl are radically different from those of a thirty-five-year-old housewife.

There is a second reason why we need to define our target-group. Not only ought groups to be homogeneous age-wise but they also ought to have a common social background. In one mission I was involved in, plans were made to reach the employees of an oil firm in the city, all of whom worked in a huge office building. It was quickly pointed out that it would be impossible to have groups comprised of both management people and office personnel even though they worked for the same firm.

Again the reason is fairly obvious. Whatever one may feel about the situation, it is a fact that such social barriers make people uneasy. Individuals are not sure how to relate to one another in the group because they have had little prior contact on the social level. Consequently, the group forms slowly, if at all.

Let me hasten to add that such barriers are not right, and within the church there must be a deliberate attempt to overcome artificial divisions. This is what Christian fellowship is all about.

But here we are speaking of outreach to non-Christians and we must face the fact that to mix a group age-wise and socially is to introduce immediate tensions, and we want to avoid this if at all possible, because for an outreach group to be effective you need a relaxed, informal atmosphere in which an individual is free to "hear" what is presented and to interact honestly.

Having said all this, let me add that it might be a fascinating experiment to draw together deliberately such a mixed group — and then use the inevitable tensions which arise as the point of contact with the real needs of the people involved. You thereby create an actual situation in which to discuss what Christ can do in the face of such tensions. However, the leader of such a group would have to be quite experienced to lead it successfully.

How then do you choose a target group? The easiest way is by asking yourself: "What group am I naturally a part of?" The answer to this question will usually be the answer to what group you ought to work with. Perhaps you will realize that your life centers around the group from the office. These are the people with whom you have unique contact and who are thereby your unique responsibility. It is self-evident that the best person to convey the Christian message to any group is someone who is himself a member of that group.

2. *Venue*

Once you have decided upon your target-group, you must consider the second factor in setting up a group, namely the *venue*. Ask yourself: "In what sort of environment do I have natural contact with this group of people? In my home? At my club? In the office? In the dormitory?" You will want to use, wherever possible, the most familiar environment for your outreach.

For example, some time ago the group with which I was working developed a real concern for the business and professional people in the city where we were based. So we decided that we would try to get through to this target group. As we thought about the problems in doing this, it became evident that we would have to pick a time when these busy men would be comparatively free. This meant lunch-time.

What then would be a natural lunch-time venue? It was quickly evident that the ideal venue would be a local hotel. Here was a familiar and attractive environment in which the men could relax. So we sent out printed invitations to a number of businessmen in the city inviting them to four consecutive Wednesday lunch-time film shows. A number of men were attracted by the idea of spending lunch-time watching a good film at this hotel. Hence we had virtually a full hall each week.

One of the most suitable of all venues is the home. In a home there are no booking fees or schedules to worry about as there would be in an hotel or hall. Even more important, the home is a familiar venue to everyone. We all live in a home, and hence we all know what is expected of us there.

Any number of venues can be used for outreach — halls, private offices, the beach, and even a cellar (which could be transformed into a "coffee-bar"). You can be creative in your choice of venue. In your consideration, do not neglect church facilities. Many churches have rooms ranging from large halls to classrooms and lounges. Used properly, particularly with individuals who have at least a nominal connection with the church, these could be just the right venue for you.

3. *Type of Group*

When you have decided upon your target-group and your venue, it is time to give your attention to the third factor, namely the *type of group* you have. Are you going to structure the evening around a dinner party or just have light refreshments? Or are you going to have a mid-morning coffee party? Or a bread and cheese lunch in the office?

Great variety is possible at this point. For example, if you have a teenage group you could hold a *barbecue and swimming party* (if you can find someone with a pool to host the evening!). A popular type of meeting for businessmen is the early morning *breakfast*. (A restaurant is booked between 6:30 and 7:30 a.m. Then over breakfast, a meeting is held, finishing in time for the men to get to work.) An easy and enjoyable way to structure an evening is around *dessert and coffee.* (Invite friends to your home after dinner and then provide a special dessert and coffee. Let your imagination go. For example, buy a gallon of ice-cream and provide five or six different flavored toppings, as well as peanuts, whipped cream, fruit, etc. When your guests arrive, hand each a large bowl and invite them to create their own mixture.)

As you will have noticed much of what I have just said has involved *food.* This is deliberate. There is something about sharing food together which breaks down barriers between people. The early Church was on to something when they structured their worship services around a shared meal.

4. *Length*

A fourth area in which a decision is required regards the *length* of the venture. Are you planning a one evening affair or will it be five weeks of Wednesday lunchtime meetings? Or perhaps you want to hold three meetings during one week — Monday, Wednesday and Friday?

There is real value in outreach on single evenings. During one city mission members of the mission staff were invited on a number of occasions into a home for an evening and then asked to speak briefly on: "Why we are doing a preaching mission in the city." This was a subject of real interest to most people (they had heard of the mission via the newspaper and radio) and so they were quite eager to come. The discussion which ensued was inevitably fascinating. This sort of one-time affair is of particular value when it comes in the context of a larger outreach effort, such as a city-wide mission.

Furthermore, such single evenings can easily turn into a series of meetings. In one city, a family invited several friends over to see a "Fact and Faith" film one evening. At the end of the evening everyone so enjoyed it, that a second evening was arranged during which some of the issues raised could be pursued at greater length. This led to a third meeting. This particular group eventually met some eight times!

Of course there is real value in setting up a series right from the start. On several occasions we have conducted Bible studies for businessmen, consisting of one lunch-time study a week for five weeks. We found that men were quite willing to commit themselves to the five weeks — if they knew in advance that it was just for five weeks. However, an open-ended invitation ("We are starting a Bible study on Tuesday. Would you like to come?") is often refused because the person does not know if he is committed for five weeks or five years!

5. *Content*

The fifth and final factor which must be considered as you set up a group is the *content* of the meeting. Will you invite in an outside guest to speak briefly and then lead a discussion? Or will you play a tape or a record of a sermon? Or will you show a film? Conduct a Bible study? Arrange a special evening of music or reading?

It is often interesting to invite in an "expert" to speak briefly to the group and then lead a discussion. However, it is not always possible (or even desirable) to bring in an outside guest. This is where tapes and records come into their own. It is possible via these media to bring world famous speakers right into your group.

A recording has many advantages. For one thing, you can *preview* what is said before the meeting — something not possible when you invite in an outside guest. If you do not feel the content is quite what is needed, you can choose another tape. Secondly, once the record has been played the group can *interact quite freely* with what has been said. If people object violently with the content, they can say so. This is not really possible when the speaker is sitting right there among you! Thirdly, there is the advantage of being able to *discuss* what has been said. We seldom have this opportunity when we hear lectures and sermons.

Films have all these advantages plus the fact that what is said is simultaneously illustrated. Furthermore, the idea of seeing a film in a home has great appeal. For example, during one mission a scientist and his wife invited to their home a group of other scientists. After a buffet meal everyone watched the "Fact and Faith" film, "Signposts Aloft." This proved to be an excellent discussion starter on the inter-relationship between science and Christianity.

It takes slightly more work to use films than it does to use tapes or records. A film must be rented and paid for, projection equipment secured, and a competent projectionist arranged for. However, it is well worth the extra effort. Films can make a deep impact on people. This is especially true in a home, because research has shown that films make much more impact on a small group than a large one. Furthermore, this same research has pointed out that a *series* of related films, shown over a period of time, tends to have a cumulative effect, and of course, a series of films is a real possibility in a home.

Thirty-five mm. slides are also useful. The really energetic group may wish to produce their own slide show. With modern cameras, extension tubes which enable re-photographing of printed pictures, and monochromatic dies which enable you to paint your own abstract slides, there is great potential for this sort of thing. You would have no trouble getting friends to attend the premier performance of your own slide show!

For young people, slides used to illustrate modern pop-music provide an interesting evening. It is quite a revelation to discover what these secular musical groups are saying about man's lostness and his search for God. A statement by such groups can then be followed by songs in the same musical idiom done by a Christian group, focusing on what is involved in finding God.[7] Teenagers would be delighted by the prospect of hearing and discussing pop music (with word-sheets or word-slides provided) after a house or beach party.

If pop music is not your taste, classical may be. On one occasion I recall spending a delightful evening with a small group of friends listening to St. Matthew's Passion, coupled with a running commentary on the music given by a young Ph.D. in Religious Music.

Today there is a wide range of Christian music which can

be used — ranging from the rock-sound of Larry Norman ("Upon This Rock") to the folk-sound of John Fischer ("The Cold Cathedral") not to mention the religiously oriented music of many secular groups (e.g. the L.P. "Jesus Christ, Superstar").

If literature is more your taste, what about an evening of readings? Some years ago my wife and I invited over a group of friends on C. S. Lewis' birthday. We celebrated with cake and coffee and then spent the evening reading aloud and discussing extracts from his many books. This same idea has since been used in evangelistic home groups, entitled: "An Evening with C. S. Lewis."[8]

In the Group Leader's Guide you will find more ideas as to what one can do in small groups. Suffice it to say that you will be limited only by the extent of your imagination. There is immense potential for such groups — groups that will not only be valuable in sharing with others what Christianity is all about, but great fun for all involved.

Key Factors in Setting Up a Group

As you plan your small group venture, you must make decisions in each of the five areas listed below. These areas are not independent. A decision in one area limits the decision in a second area. For example, if you decide that your *target group* is businessmen, then the *type of group* you hold could not be afternoon tea.

The reason for this list is to give you an idea of the scope of possibilities. Do not be limited just to these suggestions, however.

1. TARGET GROUP

Key question: What group am I a part of?

1. Teens.
2. University students.
3. Young Married Couples.
4. Thirties (single or couples).

5. Business and Professional People.
6. Retired People.
7. Relatives.
8. Neighbors.
9. Club Friends.
10. Family Friends.
11. Sportsmen.

2. VENUE

Key question: What is the natural environment for this group, or what would be an enjoyable environment?

1. Home.
2. Private Office.
3. Theater.
4. Hall.
5. Club.
6. Hotel — large or small lounge.
7. Restaurant.
8. Out-of-doors.
9. Residence Hall.
10. Church facilities.

3. TYPE OF GROUP

Key question: What will the group enjoy or what will be realistic in terms of the venue?

1. Dinner (formal, buffet, speciality — e.g. Norwegian food).
2. Coffee Morning.
3. Light Refreshments.
4. Tea.
5. Lunch Meeting (snacks, bread and cheese, each bring own lunch).
6. Barbecue.
7. Dessert and Coffee.
8. Pre-work Breakfast.
9. Banquet.
10. Garden Party.

4. LENGTH

Key question: What sort of commitment can I realistically expect?

1. One time only.
2. One time with possibility of continuing.
3. Series of ? weekly meetings.
4. Series of ? meetings during one week.
5. Weekend conference (live-in or stay at home).
6. Half-day conference.

5. CONTENT

Key question: What do I want to communicate and how can this be done in an interest-keeping fashion?

1. Guest speaker.
2. Tape Recording or Record.
3. Slide Show.
4. Film.
5. Music Evening (pop, classical, folk).
6. Literature Evening.
7. Bible Study.
8. Combination of Media.
9. Problem-centered study (e.g. How can I relate Christianity to my work?)
10. Study of a Book (e.g. *Setting Men Free*).

Prayer Is Conversation With Jesus

"To communicate Christ to others, we must communicate with Christ ourselves."

Communication with Christ implies a relationship with Him. So it must be. In our witness we are not telling others about an intriguing religious figure from the first century. We are telling them about a living Person whom we know.

But this is where the problem lies. For all sorts of reasons, we often let this relationship with Jesus dry up. We either live without any real awareness of His presence (it is possible, He does not force Himself on us); or we let our relationship with Him lapse into a set of duties which we mechanically perform.

Often the core problem is that we stop talking with Jesus. I mean this quite literally. If Jesus is a living Person (and He is, the Resurrection is a fact of history) and if He can be known by us (and He can be) then for there to be any ongoing relationship, there must be dialogue. We must speak to Him and we must listen as He speaks to us. Conversation with Jesus is the foundation of our spiritual life. In fact, it *is* our spiritual life.

Try an experiment won't you? — an experiment in conversing with Jesus.

First of all, find a place where you will be undisturbed for at least fifteen minutes. If this is not true of where you are now, find another place or wait until it is quiet. Do not try to go on until you can be alone and undistracted.

Now, get out a pen and some paper. Then read these verses slowly, listening to Jesus:

Abide in me, and I in you. As the branch cannot bear fruit by itself, unless it abides in the vine, neither can you, unless you abide in me. I am the vine, you are the branches. He who abides in me, and I in him, he it is that bears much fruit, for apart from me you can do nothing . . . If you abide in me, and my words abide in you, ask whatever you will and it shall be done for you.[9]

This is Jesus, speaking to you. Re-read this passage, listening carefully to what He is saying to you within these verses and within yourself. Write down what He says. Listen some more. Respond to Him. Let Him heal you. Let Him love you.

Share what has happened in this experiment with someone else.

Action

1. *Think about* which friends you could invite to the Outreach Evening, on the basis of the group decision as to target-group. Pray about this.

2. *Invite* the people you decide upon. When you do so, be sure to tell them just what is planned. It is important to be very open about the evening to which you are inviting them. Do not be apprehensive. If the group has done a good job in planning (as I am sure it has) the evening will be fun, relaxed, and highly profitable.

3. *Pray* for these friends (specifically, remember); for the Outreach Evening; for the group members; for yourself.

Bibliography

A. GROUP PRAYER

**1. *Praying Together; Communicating Love Through Prayer;* and *Prayer: Conversing With God* by Rosalind Rinker; Zondervan.
Clear guidelines to effective group prayer coupled with copious examples.

2. *Two or Three Together* by H. Freer and F. Hall; Harper and Row.
A manual for prayer groups, containing not only instructions but resource materials.

B. GROUPS AND THE CHURCH

*1. *Groups Alive — Church Alive* by Clyde Reid; Harper and Row.

2. *The Creative Role of Interpersonal Groups in the Church Today,* edited by John Casteel, Association Press.

3. *New Life in the Church* by Robert Raines; Harper and Row.

*4. *The Company of the Committed;* and *The Incendiary Fellowship;* by Elton Trueblood; Harper and Row.

Chapter 5

The Small Group and Witness

Group Exercises

<small>PHASE I:</small> *Group Prayer* (30 minutes)

Last week we began with a time of group prayer. So too this week. Before you pray together though, I want to mention a few more principles of group prayer, with the hope that these will make your times together even more meaningful.

1. *Pray by topics,* i.e. pray as a group about one subject until you have exhausted it. For example, you may begin by thanking God in one or two sentences, for some incident in the past week. Stop then. Another person will carry on giving thanks, followed by a third person perhaps. Then a new topic is introduced (e.g. prayer for the group). Pray about this for a while. Then move to the next topic. In this way there is a real interaction in prayer.

    Note too how prayer together in this way can almost become a conversation with God. This is different from prayer in which each person prays long prayers covering many subjects.[1]

2. *Pray in the first person when you are referring to yourself.* This is the only way to real honesty in prayer. Here is one version : "Lord, we ought to pray more often, and we ought to read our Bibles more often, forgive us." Here is the other: "Lord, forgive me. I've read my Bible only once or twice this week, and I've just prayed on-the-run, and my heart is so hungry to be with You alone. Please forgive me for this, and I put the control of my day back into Your hands."[2] However, at other times you will be praying on behalf of the whole group and hence "We" is appropriate.

3. *Pray specifically,* as we discussed last week. Not, "Lord, help me to speak more boldly," but "Lord, give me a natural opportunity next week to speak to Carol about You."

    To have more time to pray together, you will break

up into smaller groups. In these, spend a few minutes discussing topics you want to pray about. Remember especially the Outreach Evening which is coming in a few days. Some may also want to share about their experience last week in conversing with Jesus. This would be excellent — as such sharing will provide the natural basis for prayers of thanks or for prayers of intercession. Then begin praying by topics, in the first person, and specifically until your leader indicates that time is up.

PHASE II: *The Lecture* (12 minutes)

This week, as you listen to the lecture try to summarize what you consider to be the most important points which are being made.

1. _____

_____

2. _____

_____

3. _____

_____

4. _____

_____

5. _____

_____

PHASE III: *How Groups Operate* (45 minutes)

This week we are going to try a new type of group exercise: *role playing*. It works like this. An imaginary situation is set up. Certain people are assigned roles. (These roles will seldom express the person's own opinions.) The nature of each role will be defined, though the actual words to be used will not be given. The play begins. People act their parts, making up words as they go along. After a brief period of time the play is stopped, and then analyzed to see what can be learned.

Our "play" is entitled: "How not to act in a group." It is intended to illustrate the sorts of group behavior mentioned in the lecture.

The situation is this: a group of three people is studying "Witnessing Is Not Brainwashing." They begin by reading a portion from this paper (the section entitled "False Motive," p. 109 f.). Then they discuss it. Each person in the group has a role to play as indicated by the group leader.

Study Schedule

READ:

1. *The Text of the Lecture,* to understand how a successful group operates.
2. *Sections from those books in the Bibliography* which deal with aspects of this lecture which especially puzzle or interest you.

CONSIDER FOR YOURSELF:

"The Group and Me," trying to learn about your relationships in general as you analyze your relationships in the group.

ACT:

1. By *fulfilling* your responsibilities for the Outreach Evening.
2. By *praying* for those who will attend.
3. By *repairing* any broken relationships.

The Dynamics of a Small Group

"The world today is not impressed by the Bible, or by the Church, or by preaching. And we cannot confront a needy world with God's love primarily by these means. The climate of our time is one in which people listen most readily to laymen with whom they can identify."[3]

Bruce Larson

Small groups have been proclaimed by some people as "the answer" to most of the Church's ills in this century. But are they? Does one just start a group and then watch the problems melt away in the face of the dazzling love and fellowship which the group invariably generates? I think the answer is fairly obvious. We only have to recall our own experience in groups to realize that there are unsuccessful small groups as well as the successful ones I have been discussing in the past two chapters.

Groups do not automatically work. Listen, for example, to the experience of one couple with a great deal of group experience:

> Recently we visited a large Midwestern Church where our hosts, the leaders of about thirty small groups, were sold on the idea of such fellowships and what they could accomplish for their church . . . These leaders believed that if they simply gathered together to discuss their problems the Holy Spirit would be there, that the group would take fire, and that the whole community would feel its impact. But this had not happened. The enthusiasm that had carried them through the first months was dying, and the whole experiment was about to collapse.[4]

Why? What had gone wrong? In this situation, it was found that the groups had no realistic plan to follow. They just simply met. So they floundered. Groups fail for other reasons. In some it may be because certain people in the group are hindering it. Or the leader may be the problem. But the point is this: *If a group fails there is always a reason.* But, a group need not ever fail if attention is given to a few basic principles of group dynamics.

In each group there are certain forces which operate to hold it together and to give it life; or which destroy it. It is true, however, that some groups seem to function extremely well even though none of the members has ever heard of "group dynamics." But the reason these groups operate so well is that they are, in fact, paying attention to these principles, albeit intuitively. One must talk about the principles of group dynamics, not because of such successful groups, but because of the others that are floundering and failing.

> There is an important rule of thumb, tested by research: *When informed attention is paid to group processes, the chances increase that a group will be able to reach maturity and fulfil its potentialities.* On the other hand, when a group ignores the dynamic processes that influence its life, the chances increase that those dynamics may block the group at some crucial point.[5]

What then are some of these principles of group dynamics which are particularly relevant to the sort of outreach groups we are planning?

GROUPS FUNCTION ON TWO LEVELS

The first principle is this: groups function on two levels — the objective level and the subjective level — and unless these two levels complement one another the group will have problems.

The *objective side* of a group is defined by its task. That is — a group meets for a specific purpose, be it to study St. Mark's Gospel, to view a film, or to decide on the budget for next year's church program. (In your particular group, the objective reason for you meeting together is to learn how to become witnesses for Christ.)

The *subjective side* of the group relates to the inter-group relationships as well as to how each person feels as part of the group. A group is made up of people, and people have emotions and prejudices and needs and private goals. Every person in a group, at some point or other, asks himself silently: "What is my position in this group? Do the others like me? Can I really say what I think? How can I get my way? How can I get the group to see that I am brilliant, or beautiful, or witty, or kind, or spiritual?" or whatever you consider as the attribute that makes you worthy of respect. Until a person finds answers to these questions he is not really free to get on with the *task* at hand. Hence, in the guise of giving his considered opinion that the hymn books in the new church must be bright pink, he is actually asking: "Can you really accept me even with ridiculous viewpoints like this?" *Interaction within a group on the level of feelings and needs is the subjective side of group functioning.*

It is on this second level where the real problems occur. If group relationships become problematic the group is going to have a hard time getting its job done.

You will understand what I mean if you have ever noticed that some groups never seem to accomplish anything. They start out to study Isaiah 53, but then only get through the first two verses. Or they try to plan the forthcoming youth service, but after an-hour-and-a-half the only thing decided is to invite the regular organist to accompany the hymn singing.

Instead of getting on with the task in hand the group members argue with one another. Or there is a lot of horseplay. Or everyone tries to talk at once — or no one talks at all!

Why is this? What is happening in such a situation? Simply this: the group is failing to concentrate on the *task* it has because the inter-group *relationships have gone wrong.*

Hence a group, to be successful, must pay attention not only to its objective side (i.e. its task), but to its subjective side (i.e. the needs of individuals and inter-group relationships). A group which concentrates blindly on its *task* is in danger. Sooner or later, group relationships will frustrate the accomplishment of the objective goal.

Let me illustrate what I mean. A group may be studying (let us say) Mark 2. The leader declares in a rather firm and decisive tone, "Well, it is *obvious* that the first thirteen verses are *just* the story of *another healing* on Jesus' part, so consequently we can move on straight away to the rest of the chapter. Now, if you will all turn to . . ." At this point Kurt, a member of the group, interjects, in a rather exasperated tone, "But you have missed the point again. That passage is not just about a healing."

Now on the objective level this is fair enough. Kurt is right. The leader is passing too easily over a highly significant incident in Christ's revelation of Himself to the world. In a healthy group, Kurt's insights will help everyone see more clearly what Mark 2 is all about and the leader will welcome his contribution.

But in this situation, both the leader and Kurt are clashing on the subjective level. The leader is saying, by his tone and manner, as well as by his words: "I want all of you to recognize that *I* am the leader and that I can move the group in whatever direction I choose." Kurt, however, is challenging this assumption by using an error on the part of the leader to say to him: "You have done it again. You are always missing the point. You are a bad leader." In such a group, there will be real tension which will mean that much of the value of the study on an objective level is lost. The group will never get at Mark 2, because they will be so busy getting at each other!

DEALING WITH GROUP TENSIONS

It is a key principle of group dynamics that when interaction on the objective level and interaction on the subjective level are at cross purposes the group is in trouble. What can we do if we begin to sense this happening in our group?

For one thing, you must learn to detect quickly that there are problems on the subjective level. You do this by becoming aware of what others are feeling. However, these feelings will seldom be expressed directly on a verbal level. We do not *say*: "I am bored by all this." Rather we just stop taking part in the discussion. Or we slump down in our chair. Or we start staring at the trees outside the window. In each of these ways we are communicating by means other than words what we are really feelings. Be assured that the group member asleep in his chair is trying to tell the group something!

Sometimes our words even *contradict* our feelings. Take as an illustration the man "who insists in a loud voice, with his teeth clenched and his face nearly purple: 'I am not angry!' "[6]

People communicate their inner reactions in all sorts of ways — by facial expressions, gestures, tone of voice, level of attention, etc. We must learn to become sensitive to the meaning of these unspoken innuendos.

Perhaps the surest way to know what is going on in a group on the subjective level is to ask *yourself*: "What am *I* feeling right now?" If you are feeling upset, irritated, or defensive, something is wrong.

Secondly, once the problem has become apparent the only way to deal with it is to bring it out into the open. After the meeting over refreshments, you could chat with the person involved. "Peter, I felt that perhaps you were bothered by what went on tonight?" If Peter will then express what he was feeling, he can begin to cope with it. It may be possible to ask this same question while the group is still together. ("I sense that some of you are feeling upset.") What Peter is feeling, others may be feeling. Once these subjective feelings are expressed they can become of positive value to the group and they will not be destructive. It is not uncommon for the most profitable times in a group to take place when attention is shifted away from the objective to the subjective.

For example, I once read about an adult Sunday school group where this sort of thing happened. It was obvious on the particular Sunday in question that one of the girls in the group, a single school teacher, was bothered. She normally took an active part in the discussion, but on this day she was virtually silent. She seemed particularly pale and withdrawn. Finally, the leader of the group asked her if something was wrong. With that, she burst into tears and spilled out the story. Her mother with whom she lived, had just been taken to the hospital. While it appeared that the mother would probably recover, the incident had nevertheless aroused in the girl all sorts of old fears about the future and how she could cope alone in the world if her mother died. The lesson on the minor prophets that Sunday was quickly forgotten. The group which hitherto had not been particularly close was drawn together in a new way in real love and concern for the girl. During the next week people had her to dinner; others visited the mother in the hospital, etc. From this point onward, the group came alive. They began to discover one another as people. They had been transformed into a loving fellowship, whereas previously they were merely an academic study group — all because one girl had revealed her real feelings.

In this particular instance, the problem the group faced had come from outside itself, i.e. one member's mother was ill. It may, of course, happen that the problem emerges from within the group itself. An example of this is the power struggle between Kurt and the leader which was mentioned earlier. In any case, the way to cope is to bring the problem out into the open so it can be seen for what it is and then be dealt with.[7]

Almost inevitably, out of such situations which seem so potentially disruptive, we learn deeply valuable lessons — about ourselves; about relationships; about conflict; and about love and forgiveness and honesty. In other words, we learn in *experience* the meaning of the words we have hitherto just talked about. This is one of the chief values of a group.

PATTERNS OF INTERACTION

The second major principle of group dynamics is this: people will act in certain predictable ways when they are in a group. Some of these types of behavior are helpful to a group while other types hinder it. Generally, however, a form of behavior has the potential either to help or hinder a group, depending upon how it is used. Let us look at some of these types of group behavior, asking ourselves what this behavior does to a group, and how it can be dealt with if it is harmful. As you read this section keep in mind the Outreach Groups which you are going to run in the near future. This will help you understand the sort of people who will be coming into these.

In almost every group there will be the *overtalkative* person who makes long and frequent speeches and has opinions to express on every subject. Such a person can be a real help to a group, particularly if there is a vitality to his ideas. He will insure that the group keeps going. On the other hand, the overtalkative person can hinder a group by hogging too much of the time and by dominating the group. What can one do to prevent such a person from hindering the group? The leader can keep this from happening by addressing questions *by name* to other people. Or he can say: "John hold that comment for a moment and let's see what Mike and Louise feel about this." The leader may eventually, however, have to speak to the talkative person after a group session to try to help him see how he is hindering the group.

In most groups you will also find a *shy* person. For one reason or another such a person sits in the group without ever really participating. Shy people, however, are useful to a group because since they do tend to sit on the sidelines, they can thus bring an objective perspective into the midst of a heated debate — if they will, in fact, speak up. But, and this is the problem, most often they will not express themselves, so their insights are lost to the group.

Shy people may even inhibit a group. Because no one really knows what they are thinking and feeling, group sharing on a meaningful level is virtually impossible.

Shyness not only has the potential of being harmful to the group; it can also be harmful to the shy person himself. Often a person is shy because he feels he has nothing of value to contribute. But he does. Each person is valuable and has a valuable perspective which the group needs. The group must help the shy person to come to understand that his viewpoint is important. A shy person can usually be drawn out by being asked simple (though not simplistic) questions which involve the expression of an opinion or a choice. (And hence are not questions they would have difficulty in answering.)

Sometimes a normally active person withdraws from the group, and becomes an *observer*. If this happens, it usually means that the person has something on his mind. He may be upset with the group; or distracted by personal problems. The leader ought to try to draw him gently back into the group in the same way as he would a shy person.

A valuable person to have in a group is a *comic*. His "asides" and other comments may well relieve tension that has been building up, and thereby provide the humorous relief needed to give everyone a fresh perspective on the debated issue. A good laugh is immensely valuable. However, a comic can become a nuisance if he turns *everything* into a joke. His behavior then just becomes an attention-getting ploy. Furthermore, a flippant comment at the wrong moment can destroy the group atmosphere. If this happens, a chat after the group session may help the person to see that the positive value of his humor is being lost because its frequency makes it annoying.

The person with a *hidden agenda* can disrupt a group. Such a person attends a group, ostensibly to participate in the group task, but all the time he has something else on his mind which is of greater importance to him. For example, he may have a date for dinner as soon as the group finishes, and so he is eager to bring the business to an end. Or he may be more interested in showing up another member of the group whom he dislikes than in getting on with the task. It is difficult to draw such a person into the real activity of the group, unless he is willing to be honest about his preoccupations. If the leader senses someone has a "hidden agenda" he could ask (if the person can take it): "Tom, something appears to be on your mind. Should we talk about it before we try to carry on with this discussion?"

The *side-tracker* is disruptive by preventing the group from concentrating on the main issues. "That is very interesting, Mary, now what does the group think about the question at hand . . ." is one way of handling diversions. If a person persists, the leader can offer to discuss the issue after the session. Sometimes the whole group *welcomes* being side-tracked, especially if the issues being discussed are becoming challenging to them personally. Rather than face such issues, they prefer to retreat into safe side issues.

The *argumentative* type of person is often baffling to a group. Whatever is said, he seems to be "against it." Disagreement, of course, is not necessarily bad. Those who have the ability to see "the other side of the issue" can save a group from one-sidedness. But the group must feel that the opposition is genuine and not just for the sake of opposition, if such a position is to be beneficial.

Sometimes disagreement occurs simply because a person has not understood what is being said. There is always a gap between what we say and what is heard. Hence a person may be striking out against a caricature. In such cases, the group must patiently help the arguer to "hear" what really is said. Remember your exercise in reflecting-back? However, even when such a person does understand, he may still disagree. This is well and good as long as the disagreement is good-natured and done with a sincere sense of respect towards the integrity of those who are on the other side of the issue. Argument is harmful when it comes charged with emotion and with the unspoken (but nevertheless communicated) attitude: "If you disagree with me, you are an idiot." This will not happen of course if the group has developed a love and respect for one another.

GROUP ATMOSPHERE

In fact, many of these harmful behavior patterns (as well as other problems on the subjective level) will be avoided if the group atmosphere is right. If people feel warmth, love, and acceptance from a group, they will not have to argue ruthlessly or talk over much. If they feel that they will be accepted and not condemned no matter what they say, they will not have to cover up themselves by being either shy or boisterous. If the group sets the example of honest sharing, everyone will be encouraged to drop the mask behind which they hide and let their true selves be known in the group, and hence they will be opened up to the healing, redemptive love of Christ.

In other words, if the group atmosphere is right, then the group will probably not have to face severe problems with disruptive types of behavior.

What atmosphere then *do* we want to strive for? To my mind, the answer is summed up in three words: acceptance, honesty and love. Your aim is to be an *accepting* group, not a judgmental group always ready to pounce on a person's faults or wrong ideas. You also want an *honest* group — a group where real feelings and thoughts can be expressed; and hence a group where real growth can take place. Finally, you ought to aim to become a *loving* group — a group in which there is a genuine caring for one another.

1. *Acceptance*

How can a group be made into this sort of loving, accepting honest fellowship? Quite frankly, this can only come as a direct result of one's attitudes. Take, for example, acceptance and non-judgment. *As long as we consider ourselves to have "arrived" spiritually or to have special insight into God's will which few others share, we cannot help but stand in judgment of others.* We are judges (consciously or unconsciously) of any non-Christian who might come into the group because he has not yet arrived at our state of spiritual understanding. Hence, we feel that he must learn from us and that we cannot learn from him. We also stand as judges to those who are Christians, but not a part of our particular denomination (or group) because they obviously have little spiritual wisdom or they would share our perspective.

We can become a loving, accepting person only when we reach a real, experiential understanding that we too are sinners in need of grace, as are all men. It may be true that we have in the past known forgiveness from God, but this is not something which comes once only, at our conversion. We need forgiveness over and over — and not to know this is to undercut the real meaning of the Cross. Until we reach this point, we will tend to stand as judges to other people. We will see their ideas and behavior in comparision with our ideas and behavior which we consider normative. We can *only* do this because we have never really seen ourselves as God (and others too probably) sees us — with our pretense, blind spots, unadmitted failings, etc. As Bonhoeffer, the German theologian, has said: "If my sinfulness appears to me in any way smaller or less detestable in comparison with the sins of others, I am still not recognizing my sinfulness at all."[8] May God grant each of us a vision of just how deep and all pervasive this flaw called sin is in us. And may He also grant us the knowledge of how rich His forgiveness is in the face of our great need.

What happens then when we come to the point of really believing ourselves to be men with deep needs? For one thing, we can begin to allow God to meet these needs in us and hence we start to *experience* the reality of the Gospel. Second, we will start accepting all men, Christian and non-Christian, as they are — as fellow sinful creatures. Not that we accept sin therefore. On the contrary, we find a new and deep abhorrence of this cancer because we know how it destroys. Third, we find a new rapport with others because we come to them not as one who has "arrived" but as "one beggar to another" with our message of "where to find food."[9] *And we see them joyously discovering that "food."* Sam Shoemaker summed it all up when he wisely said: "It takes a sinner to catch a sinner."[10]

2. *Honesty*

Once we have seen ourselves as we really are (sinful people who are nevertheless loved by God) then we not only begin to drop our judgmental natures but we also can become honest.

We begin to develop a faculty for honesty when we become aware of our own sinful nature. As we face our real selves (and go on facing ourselves) and then allow Christ to forgive us and heal us and make us anew, we become able to live with the dark side of our personality. It is only when we cannot face this side of ourselves that we have to pretend it does not exist, and hence we are forced to be dishonest. But *we can face anything in ourselves if we have known forgiveness from God through the death of Christ.* Forgiveness wipes away the effects of the dark thing and gives us a transparency before others which is the mark of honesty.

When we have seen ourselves for what we are, and allowed Christ to deal with our sin, then we can open ourselves to others. And when we open up ourselves, others can begin to open up themselves to us. This is the first step to their own healing. "In all of his recent books Tournier (the Swiss psychiatrist) indicates that when he is personally willing to share his own faults and doubts and failures with his patients . . . and make himself vulnerable to them, healing takes place. But when he is merely professional and sits back and asks the patient to expose his problem he does not see the same results."[11]

This is why honesty is essential to a group. If we are all pretending to feel what we do not feel, or if we hide behind pious words or ideas, nothing can happen. The Holy Spirit is bound by us. The power of the Gospel is inhibited. But when we can be open, particularly with what our experience of Christ has been, life can flow.[12]

One more note. One man has written: "Transparent honesty is only possible for persons who are emotionally and spiritually healthy and mature."[13] He is, of course, right. Our outreach groups will reflect the richness — or poverty — of our spiritual experience. What this says once again is that it is top priority for each of us to devote ourselves to knowing Christ. The starting point in our attempt to be honest may have to come when we honestly admit that we know little of Christ. But once we have faced this, let us then re-solve to rectify the situation.

CONCLUSION

What I have been outlining here is the *ideal*: a group in which each person is honest and accepting; warm and out-going to all; a group in which posturing of any sort is un-necessary; a group in which the subjective and objective levels of interaction work in harmony; a group in which the needs of individuals are met and in which they come to experience the reality of the Gospel.

Of course, the *actual* can never match up to this. Your group will not be perfect, any more than you will be perfect. Or for that matter, any more than I will be perfect. I find it much easier to *write* about honesty, acceptance, and non-judgment than to *act* consistently in this fashion with my family, friends and colleagues. But this is my goal — to be-come free in Christ to be what He wants me to be.

So too, what I have outlined in these pages are *goals* (and some ideas about reaching them). They are not standards by which you must judge critically your group. They are what you aim for.

Much more could be said about setting up and running small groups. However, the way you will learn most about conducting small groups is by being a part of small groups yourself. Your own experience in groups is your best text-book. All I can do is to give you some idea of how to start and what to watch for.

The Group and Me

You have been in a group now for some five weeks. It is time to stop and take stock of how you fit into the group and what your relationships are with the others. This will be a valuable exercise in that often our relationships with others in a group mirror our relationships with people in general.

1. What sort of group member are you? Check those descriptive phrases below which best describe how you act in your small group.

   (a) Shy . . . ————————
   (b) Overtalkative . . ————————
   (c) Argumentative . . ————————
   (d) Witty . . . ————————
   (e) Aggressive . . . ————————
   (f) Passive . . . ————————
   (g) Looking on . . . ————————
   (h) Silent . . . ————————
   (i) Theorizing . . . ————————
   (j) Leading . . . ————————
   (k) Summarizing . . . ————————
   (l) Bored . . . ————————
   (m) Enthusiastic . . . ————————
   (n) Fearful . . . ————————
   (o) Baffled . . . ————————
   (p) Hostile . . . ————————
   (q) Other . . . ————————
   (r) Other . . . ————————

2. Why are you this sort of person? ————————————
   ——
   ——
   ——

3. Would you like to change? If so, what sort of group member would you like to be? _____

_____

_____

4. How can you become this? _____

_____

_____

5. How do you think others in this group view you?

_____

_____

6. Do you have problems in relating to anyone in the group? Why? (e.g. "I can't seem to get along with John. He is just too pushy.")

_____

_____

_____

7. What can you do to improve these relationships?

_____

_____

_____

8. How would you rate yourself as an honest person?

_____

_____

_____

9. How would you rate yourself as an accepting person?

_____

_____

_____

10. If you dared to be totally honest with one other person, what would you share?

_____

_____

_____

11. What have you learned from your relationship in the group about your relationships to your family? Your friends? Your colleagues? _____

_____

_____

_____

_____

_____

Action

1. *Fulfill your responsibility* for the Outreach Evening, e.g. make sure you have made the salad, or secured the extra chairs.

2. *Pray for those* who are coming with you to the Outreach Evening. Pray specifically and in expectation.

3. *Fix up any strained relationships* in the group (as far as you can) which became apparent as you worked on "The Group and Me" exercise. Try to do this before the Outreach Evening takes place.

Bibliography

A. GROUP DYNAMICS

1. *Introduction to Group Dynamics* by G. & H. Knowles; Association Press.
2. *Learning to Work in Groups* by Matthew Miles; Columbia University Press.
3. *Learning Together in the Christian Fellowship* by Sara Little; John Knox Press.

B. LEADING GROUPS

1. *Leading Bible Discussions* by James Nyquist; Inter-Varsity Press.
2. *How to Start a Neighborhood Bible Study* by M. Kunz and C. Schell.
3. *Know How to Lead Bible Study and Discussion Groups* by J. Hills Cotteril and M. Heines; Scripture Union.

Chapter 6

The Content of Witness (Part 1)

The Content of Witness (Part 1)

Group Exercises

PHASE I: *The Lecture — Part 1* (5 minutes)

We are changing the order of the session this evening. The lecture has been split into two parts, each of which will be followed by a group exercise related to it. Now as you listen to Part 1, takes notes on the question:

How can we evaluate the effectiveness of a group?

1.
2.
3.
4.
5.

PHASE II: *Evaluating Our Group Outreach* (30 minutes)

Answer the following questions quickly (four minutes). They will serve as a basis for discussion.

1. How would you rate the Outreach Evening in terms of:
   (a) Interest Level _____

   _____

   (b) Communication _____

   _____

   (c) Value _____

   _____

2. Describe the atmosphere of the evening _____

   _____

3. How did you feel personally:
   (a) Before the meeting _____

   _____

(b) During it _____

_____

(c) Afterwards _____

_____

4. What were the best parts of the evening? _____

_____

5. What parts did not go well? _____

_____

6. What can be done to improve matters? _____

_____

7. What lessons did you learn? _____

_____

PHASE III: *The Lecture — Part II* (10 minutes)

Answer these questions while listening to the lecture. You will then use your answers in the Phase III exercise.

1. What do you want to communicate to others about Jesus?

2. Who is Jesus?

3. What has He done?

4. How do we respond to Him?

PHASE IV: *Who Jesus Is* (40 minutes)

This will be an exercise in trying to put into clear, concise words just who Jesus is. To do this, the group will be split up into sub-groups of three. In each triad, one member will be chosen as a "Christian," a second as an "interested non-Christian," while the third is the "observer."

The "Christian" then will try to explain to the "non-Christian" who Jesus is. A word of warning: this is not an exercise in argument! The "non-Christian" is not an antagonist who will ask difficult or peripheral questions (e.g. "That's well and good, but what about evolution?"). The purpose of the exercise is not to *convince* another who Jesus is, but rather to *inform* him. The "non-Christian" really wants to know and his questions ought to reflect this. Try also to have a genuine *dialogue*. The job of the "non-Christian" is to get the "Christian" to express himself clearly and accurately.

During the first run, the "non-Christian" will begin with the words: "Tell me now, who is Jesus?" and the "Christian" will seek to explain — *without* discussing either the work of Jesus or the personal significance of His life. In other words, he is to concentrate on the first point of the outline given in the lecture.

While the dialogue carries on, the observer ought to be making notes. Is the "Christian" clear in his explanation? Does he rely on jargon? Is he accurate? To the point? When the dialogue is complete, the observer will lead a discussion as to its effectiveness.

In run two, the "Christian" will seek to communicate what Jesus did; while in run three the "Christian" will point out what the work of Christ means to the individual. Therefore, each run is different; each starting where the last left off.

This may well prove difficult at first, so do not be overly frustrated if you find yourself hard put as the "Christian" to express what you mean. Rather, allow this frustration to lead you to more study and practice.

READ:

1. *The Text of the Lecture,* asking two questions: "What were *my* emotional reactions to the Outreach Evening?" and "How can I communicate Christ to my friends?"
2. *The Supplementary Paper,* "Verbal Witness," assessing your conversation with others in terms of these principles.
3. *Sections from those books in the Bibliography* which deal with aspects of this lecture which especially puzzle or interest you.

CONSIDER FOR YOURSELF:

"A Dialogue About Jesus."

ACT:

1. *By discussing* who Jesus is with someone.
2. *By keeping contact* with the friends that came to the Outreach Evening.

The Content of Witness (Part 1)

Jesus — the Focus of Our Witness

> *"During the Tell-Scotland campaign in the mid-fifties, a minister from the north wrote to the organizers at the movement's headquarters in Glasgow. 'We have our committees organized, our literature prepared, our schedules set, our promotion underway. We are ready now to take part in "Tell Scotland." But, pray tell me, what are we to tell Scotland?' "*[1]
>
> *Leighton Ford*

This past week you had your first experience of small-group evangelism. I hope this was a really good experience for you — so much so that you are now feeling more excited than ever to get on with the whole outreach program. I know though that for most of you this first experience had its moments of personal trauma. Our emotions are funny things especially when we go into any new experience. Hence I think it would be of value to look briefly at some of these feelings to see what they really mean and what we can learn from them.

OUR EMOTIONS IN OUTREACH

1. *Apprehension*

I suspect that one feeling most of you had when you were planning the outreach group was apprehension. I can remember a group of five lay people who had enthusiastically planned some home meetings for teenagers during one mission. These people launched into the whole scheme of home evangelism with real gusto. However, two days before the first meeting they all had a full-blown case of nerves. "What have we let ourselves in for?" seemed to express most adequately the group sentiment. Well, the long planned but now dreaded night arrived and I am happy to report that each of the five survived the experience! Not only that, they enjoyed it immensely. So did all who came (others did actually

168

show up, to the group's amazement). Furthermore, everyone was looking forward to the next session.

We have to face the fact that as human beings we generally *fear* any new situation. The reason for this is simple enough — because the situation is new, we cannot anticipate what will happen. When we cannot anticipate, then we begin to *imagine* all that could go wrong. Thoughts flash through our minds: "What am I doing in this situation? Do I really have anything to say to others? Am I just making a fool out of myself? Will I ever be able to face the Browns again since they have actually agreed to come? Perhaps I can get sick? What if no one comes? Or talks? Or enjoys himself?" and so our imagination roams.

In all this remember: first, that such fears are quite natural. We all experience them. The important thing is not to give in to our fears by opting out of the fear-provoking situation. Second, only a fraction of what you fear could actually take place! Furthermore, if one fear is realized, it makes a whole host of other fears impossible. For example, if as you fear, no one comes to the group, then your fear about not having enough to eat cannot be realized!

Third, many of our fears are based on wrong assumptions. For example, we fear no one will be interested in Christianity. But this is not so. In our work we have found exactly the opposite, namely that most people are deeply interested in Christianity as long as they are not hammered into listening. Your friends will *welcome* the opportunity you offer them to come to the group.

Fourth, do remember that whatever does happen can be made into a good and profitable experience. All things *do* work together for good for those who love God[2] — if only we will let this happen. I remember one small group in which no outsiders did, in fact, show up. So the small band of Christians who found themselves alone in what was meant to be an outreach group, used the time to ask *why* no one came. This resulted in a most profitable discussion. They recognized certain mistakes they had made. Then they went on to lay better plans for the next attempt. Finally they prayed together for the forthcoming meeting. As a result of their planning and prayer, their next attempt was highly successful. Often though we let the "failure" discourage us: "Oh, well, I knew it wouldn't work" and we never try again.

Fifthly, we become apprehensive when we fail to rely on the fact that it is God who has called us to such outreach attempts and that hence He is with us in our every effort, and that He will use whatever happens.

2. *Discouragement*

If apprehension is the emotion that assails us before the event, then discouragement is our enemy afterwards. On one occasion, a couple planned an outreach evening in their home. They duly invited friends, arranged a film, and purchased food. The evening was held. I saw the hostess the next day and found her deeply discouraged. "How did it go?" I asked. "Not very well at all," she said. "I don't think anyone was really satisfied." But later that day, she called on the friends who had been at her home. To her utter amazement, they all had had a marvelous time. In fact, they asked when they could come for another such meeting. The long and the short of all this is that her assessment was 100 percent wrong and the one-time outreach evening eventually became eight meetings held over the next three months.

Discouragment comes when what happens falls short of, or is different from, what we expected. We expect six couples and only four actually come. So we have failed. Or during the discussion only one or two people seem to have understood the point of the tape recording. Hence we feel that we have failed.

But is this "failure"? Hardly, all it really says is that we cannot ever know beforehand just what will take place. You plan for twelve and only eight come. Was the evening insignificant for the eight? It *seemed* as if only one or two understood, but how can you know what the rest actually heard?

If you ever do feel discouraged, remember first, that numbers are not an infallible measure of success. A meeting of 2,000 is by no means automatically a more significant meeting than one of five people.

Second, do not measure success or failure on the basis of your own interpretation. The probem may be that your anticipation was faulty. Third, get rid of the success/failure mentality. In God's eyes the question is: Have you done the best you could? Fourth, remember that you seldom can really know what is happening within another person. At times the least expected things make the deepest impact upon others.

Then finally, *learn* from your real mistakes (you will make some). Do not let them discourage you. Mistakes are not tragedies, they are opportunities for learning. It is interesting that the Communists have this philosophy. After each campaign they hold what is called an "inquest" at which their sole concern is to discover what mistakes they made. In such a session:

> When you make a contribution to the discussion, you first criticize yourself, admitting that it was in such-and-such a way that you went wrong. You make no reference to your successes. These can be taken for granted. . . . You point out where (others) went wrong too. . . . Every mistake is brought to the surface. But, more important, persistent probing reveals why the mistakes were made, how they might have been avoided and how the lessons learned from them can be applied to specific forms of activity which are already planned. . . . One of (the inquest's) most important consequences is that the teachers feel free to send members into action without being inhibited by the thought that they may make mistakes. For they already know that mistakes need not be disastrous, provided that all concerned study them in due course, learn from them and try to ensure that they are not repeated.[3]

While this method is too harsh in its application (because it springs from a different view of man than Christians hold), it does point out that mistakes are not to be feared — but to be used for learning.[4]

3. *Unexpected Difficulties*

There is yet another factor to be taken into account. It is just this: if your group has the potential to make a real impact upon others, you must anticipate that you will experience unexpected difficulties, often arising from the least expected sources. I say this because of a pattern which I have seen emerge around the ministry of a group of which I was a part for years. Every time we were about to launch a new outreach effort, problems crowded in upon us. Our relationships with one another became problematic; or we all experienced unusual and uncharacteristic depression; or we were called to help in a crisis in someone's life which sapped time and energy.

I noticed this same sort of phenomenon at several university missions we conducted. In each, just when things were going well, the executive committee began to fall apart. In two cases, key committee members were hauled before their faculty advisors and told to drop immediately all outside activity as they were in danger of failing. (Both had previously received A's, and both did ultimately pass very easily.) The week before the main lecture series on one campus, despite excellent response to early mission activities, the whole committee was depressed. Other things had crowded in — boy friend trouble, family crises, etc.

Why all this? Problems are part of living — but why the sudden spate, affecting so many people, at such a crucial time? I feel the answer is wrapped up in St. Paul's assertion that ". . . we are not contending against flesh and blood, but against the principalities, against the powers; against the world rulers of this present darkness; against the spiritual hosts of wickedness in the heavenly places."[5] As Christians we take the supernatural seriously — both the divine and the demonic. We believe that this world is, in fact, in the grip of the dark powers and hence it is reasonable to expect that we will have to face demonic opposition if we start to rock the boat and actually get out and win others to Jesus Christ. As C. S. Lewis has put it, "There is no neutral ground in the universe; every square inch, every split second, is claimed by God and counterclaimed by Satan."[6]

Hence our need to go into outreach groups with an awareness, born through prayer, of God's presence and of His victorious power. Incidentally, in no situation have such unanticipated problems actually ruined an effort (though I suppose they could have done this were we to throw in the sponge as a result of the pressure). They just made the going tougher.

4. *Success*

One more word is in order for those of you who are baffled by what I have been saying because you had no fear, no discouragement, or no particular problems — but did have a superb time in your first outreach group. It is not for you, of course, that I have been writing thus far. What I have written is for those who did go through such emotion. It is important to point out these things because if we are caught unaware by our emotions, there is the temptation to give up, when in fact this is the last thing we must do. However, I suspect that as you keep on in your outreach efforts you will face some of what I have mentioned. But for the time being, just file this section away in your mind as material to be referred to in case of future need!

THE CONTENT OF OUR WITNESS

As plans were being made for the Outreach Evening one question which I imagine was raised in the minds of many is this: "When you get right down to it, just what is it we want to communicate to non-Christians?" This, of course, is a terribly important question. It is almost the most important question in the whole course. Without a clear, sure grasp of our *message,* all discussion of *method* is ultimately futile. What then is our message? What is the content of our witness?

To answer this, let us look at St. Peter's first sermon, given on the Day of Pentecost to explain to the crowds the meaning of the strange events they had just witnessed. He summarized his whole sermon with these words: "Now therefore the whole nation of Israel must know beyond the shadow of a doubt that this Jesus, whom you crucified, God has declared to be both Lord and Christ."[7]

When Peter explained Christianity he focused on one thing: Jesus Christ. Herein is the heart of our message as well. *Our aim in witness, ultimately, is to help others come face to face with the Living Christ in all His magnificence.* Witness that focuses on the Church, the Christian ethic, or even on one's personal experience of Christ (either currently or in the past at conversion) is incomplete — because a man becomes a Christian not by joining an organization, subscribing to an ideology, or hearing of another man's experience. He becomes a Christian when, with a sense of personal need, he confronts Christ. All witness, therefore must ultimately center on Jesus.[8]

In particular our witness ought to focus on three questions:

1. Who is Jesus?
2. What has He done?
3. What does this mean for individuals?

1. *The Person of Jesus*

First of all, we must focus on the person of Jesus. There is a great deal of confusion today over just who this remarkable man is. Some are content to explain Him as merely a great teacher — an articulate idealist with new conceptualizations to offer mankind. Others see Jesus as a prophet — as a seer with deep insight into the workings of man and nature and hence one able to predict accurately. Still others seek to understand Jesus as a man of God — that is, as one with an exceptionally clear understanding of the supernatural and a deep, pious commitment to it. However, none of these descriptive titles, accurate though they are, tell us the whole story.

No, Jesus Himself claimed to be more than a teacher or a

prophet or a man of God. He in fact called Himself "the Son of God." As C. S. Lewis has pointed out:

> Jesus said: "I am the begotten of the One God, before Abraham was, I am," and remember what the words "I am" were in Hebrew. They were the name of God, which must not be spoken by any human being, the name which it was death to utter. . . .
>
> If you had gone to Buddha and asked him, "Are you the son of Brahma?" he would have said: "My son, you are still in the vale of illusion." If you had gone to Socrates and asked, "Are you Zeus?" he would have laughed at you. If you had gone to Mohammed and asked, "Are you Allah?" he would first have rent his clothes and then cut your head off. If you had asked Confucius, "Are you Heaven?" I think he would have probably replied: "Remarks which are not in accordance with nature are in bad taste."[9]

Jesus set Himself apart from all other prophets and teachers by the magnitude of His claims. *We must understand this fact if we are ever to come to Him.* We dare not avoid the issue.

> "I am ready to accept Jesus as a great moral teacher, but I don't accept His claim to be God." That is the one thing we must not say. A man who was merely a man and said the sort of things Jesus said would not be a great moral teacher. He would either be a lunatic — on a level with the man who says he is a poached egg — or else he would be the Devil of Hell. You must make your choice. Either this man was, and is, the Son of God: or else a madman or something worse. You can shut Him up for a fool, you can spit on Him and kill Him as a demon; or you can fall at His feet and call Him Lord and God. But let us not come with any patronizing nonsense about His being a great human teacher. He has not left that open to us. He did not intend to.[10]

Who then is Jesus? "Jesus is God," is the answer most simply stated. Jesus is God-come-in-the-flesh, at a certain point in human history for a specific purpose, namely to make it possible for man, the rebel against God, to end that rebellion.

It is important that a man know just who Jesus is for only then can he come to Him, in all confidence, as his Savior.

If you are clear and articulate in your witness, it is at this point that your friends will stop and say: "Wait a minute. You can't ask me to believe that! What proof is there that Jesus is actually who He claims to be?" This is a fair question and one which everyone must face if his mind is to be committed to Christ as well as the rest of his being.

There is, of course, substantial proof to the mind of a genuine inquirer that Jesus is indeed God incarnate. Suffice it to say that the ultimate verification of Jesus' claim to deity comes via the historical event of the resurrection. If you are interested in pursuing the facts behind this assertion, I would recommend that you read one of the books in the bibliography. In particular, John Stott's volume, *Basic Christianity,* gives a splendid, concise survey of the evidence surrounding Jesus' claim to deity.

2. *The Work of Jesus*

Our understanding of Jesus is not complete, however, until we ask ourselves the second question: "For what purpose did this God-man come to our planet?"

He came, of course, to teach us. But important though His teaching is, *He came primarily to die.* Herein lies the ultimate reason for His visit to our planet. He came to die to make it possible for men to be forgiven and hence to come into fellowship with God.

His death was necessary to overcome the barrier that existed between God and man, as a result of man's choice to live his life apart from God. When man chose to go it alone, a spoiling effect called sin entered his life, making him into a creature unable to know God in a personal way. Through Christ's death, the spoiling effect of sin was reversed. Man could be forgiven. Man could know God. Thus St. Peter said: "Christ died for sins once for all, the righteous for the unrighteous, that He might bring us to God."[11]

A great deal more could be said about the atonement.

Volume after volume has been written in an attempt to plumb the depths of its meaning. Yet all that is necessary for us to know and to believe is that because Christ died, we can come back to God and be forgiven. Do not complicate your witness by trying to expound theories about the atonement, as you run the risk of obscuring the obvious and glorious fact that by Christ's death we can come to God. As C. S. Lewis put it:

> People ate their dinners and felt better long before the theory of vitamins was ever heard of: and if the theory of vitamins is some day abandoned they will go on eating their dinners just the same. Theories about Christ's death are not Christianity: they are explanations about how it works . . .
>
> We are told that Christ was killed for us, that His death has washed out our sins, and that by dying He disabled death itself. That is the formula. That is Christianity. That is what has to be believed. Any theories we build up as to how Christ's death did all this are, in my view, quite secondary: mere plans or diagrams to be left alone if they do not help us, and even if they do help us, not to be confused with the thing itself.[12]

3. *Response to Jesus*

The third question is: "What does all this mean to us personally? Does a man thus become a Christian when he comes to accept that Jesus is the Son of God, the One who died in order to make it possible for him to come to God? The answer is "No," if this is merely a matter of intellectual belief on his part. Becoming a Christian is not a matter of saying: "Yes, I believe those doctrines," no matter how correct the doctrines may be. Becoming a Christian is a matter of entering into a *personal relationship with Christ,* as a result of our belief.

The first step in becoming a Christian comes when a man realizes with sorrow that he has been living his life apart from God; when he sees that the controlling desire in his life has been his own self interest. The second step comes when he reaches the point of believing that because Christ, the Son of

God, died on a cross, in some mysterious way this has made it possible for him to come into a vital relationship with God. The third step in this process involves an act of commitment. The man, on the basis of his trust in Christ, in the face of his longing to know God, gives himself to Christ to be His loyal follower. By an act of the will he says to Christ: "Yes, I open my life to You. I ask for forgiveness for my past rebellion. I desire now that You become my Lord and my Master."

A splendid *picture* of what this sort of commitment is all about is given us by John in the book of Revelation. He asks us to imagine Christ standing outside a house (which is a symbol of our life) saying: "Behold, I stand at the door and knock; if any one hears my voice and opens the door, I will come in to him and eat with him, and he with me."[13] Christian commitment is just that. It is asking Christ to come into our life. In his gospel, John describes what happens when we in fact open the door of our life to Christ. "But to all who received him (Christ), who believed in his Name, he gave power to become children of God."[14]

SUMMARY

It is difficult to set down a pattern of Christian commitment and then say: "This is how it always happens." God's Spirit is far greater than any of our formulations. He deals with each man in His own way in accord with who that man is. We dare not presume to articulate a plan and then judge every man's experience by it.

Yet on the other hand, even though men come to God in such diverse ways, there do seem to be common elements in each experience. There is, for example, the awareness of the person of Christ, i.e. there is the sense that we have entered into a vital, real experience with another personality.

If a man's Christianity is only a matter of doctrine i.e. of certain ideas which he holds, he has yet to come into the fullness of Christian experience. Belief is necessary but not sufficient. It is the beginning of conversion. The consummation comes when he discovers the glorious reality of the Christ who stands behind the doctrine.

A second common element is the apprehension and trust that we are able to come into such a relationship, *because Christ died and rose again.* One's understanding of the atonement may be absolutely minimal (hopefully it will grow over the years), but there ought to be the sense that when Christ died, He died for me and hence enabled me to know Him.

A third common element in Christian conversion is the desire to know God. No one can come to Christ unless he wants to. There must be in a man a sense of being cut off from God, coupled with a desire to come back to God, and a willingness to give up (by God's grace) his self-centered style of life.

Finally, there is a resolve to follow Christ, coupled with the awareness (however shadowy) that this is not always going to be easy. Christ will make demands upon him.

Of course thus far I have been looking at conversion from the point of view of the man who is being converted. There is the other side — God's point of view. As we draw near to Him, He is at the same time drawing near to us. As we reach out in faith, He is reaching for us.

Jesus is the focus of our witness. It is He we want to share with our friends. As Christians, we must therefore learn how to do so, in a clear, gentle and natural way. May God grant you the ability to press on until you can do this. This is what witness is all about.

The Content of Witness (Part 1)

A Dialogue About Jesus

During the group session you had a chance to try your hand at communicating to another person just who Jesus is. In this exercise, do this very same thing, except in written form: that is, write out an imaginary dialogue in which a Christian explains to an interested non-Christian who Jesus is, what He has done, and what this means to a person. Be sure to cover each of these three points.

Assume that the non-Christian has no objections, but is just ignorant about Jesus.

If possible, first read over the paper by Bruce Larson, "Verbal Witness" (the Supplementary Reading for this chapter). Try to apply what he says in your dialogue.

This dialogue will not only give you a chance to think about and write out your answer to this key question. It will also help you to think about the sorts of questions non-Christians actually have about Jesus.

Action

1. *Discuss who Jesus is* with someone this week. The dialogue you have written out will provide the framework for this.

2. *Pray about such an opportunity.* Then be sensitive to situations. One man I know, after doing the exercises in this chapter, found himself at a Bible-study group for businessmen — in which only three people turned up! They could not do the study planned. So he said: "We did an interesting exercise this week at a training group I attend. We tried to put into words who Jesus is. We could do the same thing now. Interested?" They were, and not just academically. He found as they talked that one of the men was desperately seeking the answer to this very question.

   It is best, of course, to discuss who Jesus is with someone seeking this answer. But it may be that you will have to do this with your spouse, or a Christian friend. But this is all right. It will still serve as a means of gaining experience and confidence if no other natural opportunity emerges.

3. *Pray for those who attended the Outreach Evening.* What is your further responsibility to them? How can you follow-up their interests, or their needs?

4. *Follow-up* these friends.

The Content of Witness (Part 1)

Verbal Witness

By Bruce Larson

Witness at some point must be verbal. Here are some ingredients I consider important for verbal communication.

1. *Be intriguing, intelligent and relevant when you speak about Jesus Christ.* A pious tone or artificial words do not communicate the reality of Christian faith.

2. *Use the language of the other person.* We must remember that the original Greek of the New Testament was the language of the street, not the language of scholars. Elizabethan English, the language of the King James Bible, is not the language that people use today. The truths of the Bible are much greater than any attempt, past or present, to describe them. We must learn to use the language of our day, to speak about eternal truths, even as Jesus and the first-century apostles did.

3. *Be enthusiastic and sincere when you witness.* This certainly cannot be artificially generated. When we are genuinely enthusiastic about who Christ is, what He has done for us, and what He can do for another, effective communication takes place.

4. *Try to start with a point of agreement.* Even someone hostile to God or the Church will say something with which we can agree. When one preacher I know got into conversation with a man who professed to be an atheist, he said: "Tell me about the god you don't believe in. Perhaps I don't believe in him either." That was a starting point for relevant communication.

5. *Express a part of your own needs or of God's answer which somehow touches on the other person's condition.* "Total recall" is unnecessary and will only bore him. Tell that part of your experience that most nearly matches the place where he is struggling right now.

6. *Ask questions.* This helps the person to talk through his own doubts and fears, as well as his hopes and

aspirations. Remember that Jesus was a master in the use of questions.

7. *Help him to clarify his needs,* to get behind his hurt or jealousy or resentment and tell you what this has triggered in him to make him bitter or depressed at the moment. This enables the person to understand himself and to find a beginning point in his own life where God's answers may apply.

8. *Do not assume anything.* The person is neither as good nor as bad as he appears to be. Find out what he really believes and feels, and what he wants for his life. One of the best questions might be, "What do you most want to get out of life?" This can disarm even a militant atheist, who may begin to share his aspirations with you. In the same way, do not assume that because someone is a church member he believes all the things his church teaches. By assuming nothing, we let the person speak for himself and clarify his own position in our presence.

9. *Do not criticize the person for what he is doing or saying.* Try to guide him into some kind of helpful approach that will help him be the person he has told you he wants to be.

10. *Help him to make a decision.* After he has talked through his problems, hopes and fears, help him to find a beginning point where he can trust God. It may be an initial decision to turn his life over to Christ, or it may be some next step that will let God take him deeper into the Christian life. Try to pray *with* him, rather than *for* him. Ten words of prayer from him in your hearing will mean more to him than an hour's sermonizing or teaching from you.

11. *Follow up on this friend frequently in the days that follow.* Have lunch with him, call him, write to him, put him in touch with others if he does not live near you. Let him know that God cares and that you care. Encourage him to write to you or to call you often. Let him know that there will be discouragements and

setbacks but that these are normal and he should not fear them.*

Bibliography

COMMUNICATING THE GOSPEL

1. *A Short Life of Christ* by Everett F. Harrison; Wm. Eerdmans and Co.
**2. *Basic Christianity* by John Stott, IVF Press.
   A historical study of the person of Jesus.
**3. *Mere Christianity* by C. S. Lewis; Fontana Books.
4. *Have You Considered Him* by Wilbur Smith; IVF Press.
   A most interesting booklet introducing the fascinating personality of Jesus.
5. *Jesus As They Saw Him* by William Barclay, SCM Press.
   A study of the titles of Jesus.
6. *Jesus and His Story* by Ethelbert Stauffer; Alfred Knopf Publishers.
   A study of the amazing evidence about Jesus drawn from non-Biblical sources.

*From *Setting Men Free* (Grand Rapids: Zondervan Publishing House, 1967). pp. 61-63.

Chapter 7

The Content of Witness (Part 2)

The Content of Witness (Part 2)

Group Exercises

PHASE I: *Our Spiritual Pilgrimage* (40 minutes)

Part 1:

This week the lecture deals with the question of how a man becomes a Christian. As an introduction to this, think through your own spiritual experience. When did you first become aware of God? When was your faith most vital? Least vital? Then in the squares below, draw a graph, a sketch, a design, etc. describing how you have travelled in your spiritual pilgrimage. Indicate the high and the low points as well as where you are now. For example:[1]

Think about your own experience and sketch it below. Take ten minutes.

Part 2:

Now think about the point at which you became a follower of Christ. Describe this, in words or by a sketch. You may have had a dramatic conversion experience as an adult. If so, what led you to this? Or you may have always tried to follow Christ. If so when did you really become aware of His presence.

Part 3:

Share either Part 1 or 2 with the person you have been paired with. The role of the listener will be to help you articulate clearly your experience of Christ.

PHASE II: *The Lecture* (12 minutes)

How does a man become a Christian? Make notes as you listen to the lecture. These then will serve as the basis for the next exercise.

The Content of Witness (Part 2)

PHASE III: *Becoming a Christian* (35 minutes)

Once again you have split up into groups of three. This week you will continue your dialogue with the "interested non-Christian." His question this time is: "How can I become a Christian?" The "Christian" ought to try to answer this in words the average non-Christian will understand.

Study Schedule

READ:

1. *The Text of the Lecture* to learn how to help another person become a Christian.
2. *The Supplementary Paper,* "The Art of Introduction" thinking as you read it of introducing Jesus to one of your friends.
3. *Sections from those books in the Bibliography* which deal with aspects of this lecture which especially puzzle or interest you.

CONSIDER FOR YOURSELF:

"*A Dialogue About Commitment*" in order to learn how to express to someone else how to become a Christian.

ACT:

1. *By sharing Christ* with others.
2. *By practicing* explaining to a friend how to become a Christian.

Introducing Others to Jesus

"The longer I live the more sure I become that nearly everyone needs the jolt and shock of a deep challenge and a real conversion. Behind the 'But I always have had faith' attitude lies often great pride: and the sign of it may be this person's powerlessness to get faith across to anyone else."[2]

Samuel Shoemaker

In this chapter I want to continue our discussion of the content of our witness. In particular I want to discuss the question of how a man who has come to believe that Jesus is the Son of the living God can in fact translate these intellectual convictions into the experience of coming to know Jesus Christ. The key question in this chapter is: "How can a man become a real Christian?"

In particular I want to look at this question through the eyes of the man who is outside the Church. How can we communicate how to become a Christian in such a way that he will really understand what we are saying? This will mean of course, that we will have to translate the theological jargon which we as Christians use, into more familiar words which are easily understood by the proverbial "man-in-the-street."[3] However, to "translate" the Gospel into non-theological terms, we must first have a fairly clear understanding of what the Gospel actually is in theological terms. This is what we shall discuss first.

A THEOLOGICAL STATEMENT OF THE GOSPEL

As a basis for this theological statement of the Gospel let us consider Mark 1:14-17, in which we find spelled out in bold, clear terms what is involved in becoming a Christian.

> Now after John was arrested, Jesus came into Galilee, preaching the Gospel of God, and saying, "The time is fulfilled, and the kingdom of God is at hand; *repent, and believe in the Gospel.*" And passing along by the Sea of Gali-

lee, he saw Simon and Andrew the brother of Simon casting a net in the sea; for they were fishermen. And Jesus said to them, "Follow me and I will make you become fishers of men!"

There are three key elements in this statement:

1. Repentance.
2. Belief in the Gospel.
3. Following Christ.

Herein lies the essence of Christian commitment.

1. *Repent*

To repent means literally "to change one's mind." In the Mark 1 passage, Jesus links repentance with the Kingdom of God. He was saying: "Change your mind about God." But why? Why do we need to change our mind about God? Simply because, as someone has put it: "We have all repudiated the living and true God and have gone into the God-business for ourselves." In other words, ". . . we decide to run our own lives, choose what we want, and make up our own minds about what is right and wrong. . . . This is broadly what the Bible means by sin. It is refusing God the right to be God in our life. What we generally regard as 'sins' (stealing, lying etc.) are simply the signs that we have pushed God out."[4]

To repent means that we change our minds about this state of affairs. We decide that we no longer want to live life without God. We decide that we do want God to become the center of our being.

Repentance involves therefore a sorrow or *regret* over the past when we tried to live without God. We are deeply saddened as we look back and see what our selfishness has done — to others and to ourselves. Repentance also involves the *resolve* to live a new sort of life in the future with God's help.

At this point, we might well ask: "But what is wrong with living a life apart from God? So what?" We are, of course, free to live without God. God, in His incredible sovereignty, has allowed us this option. We are not puppets. But the fact is that to live apart from God is to live a half-life. God our Creator made us not only physical but spiritual beings. He made us to need not only food, air and sleep, but also fellowship with Himself. Without the sense of God's presence in our life, a vital part of our nature is literally dead. Our nature is flawed and our life forever bears this stamp of imperfection.

We all know this, at least in the sense that we are aware that something is wrong with us. We may not be able to define what is wrong. We may be totally unaware that our basic problem is our dead spiritual selves. Yet we do still *experience* the fact that something is missing.

> This separation from God shows up differently with different people. The disease is the same, the symptoms vary. Sometimes there is guilt, or lack of meaning in life, or emptiness; at other times one senses a lack of personal self-control or impure thoughts.[5]

At the core of our being, something is radically wrong — *and we know it.*

Repentance marks the first step in dealing with this "wrong." It involves an *understanding* of what the "wrong" is — i.e. a lack of God's presence; a *regret* over what our selfishness has resulted in; and a *resolve* to become what we were meant to be, by God's grace. However, repentance is only the first step. In and of itself, it has no power — either to confer forgiveness for the past or to guarantee a better life in the future. If we stop here, we have done nothing more than make yet another "good resolution." This is why our Lord follows the command to repent with the charge to "believe the Gospel." Repentance indicates our willingness to change. The Gospel gives us the power to do so.

2. *Believe the Gospel*

   a. What is the Gospel?

We are told to "believe the Gospel." But what is this

"Gospel" (literally "good news") that we are to believe? St. Paul sums it up succinctly in First Corinthians 15:1-6:

> Now I would remind you, brethren, in what terms I preached to you the gospel, which you received, in which you stand, by which you are saved. . . . For I delivered to you as of first importance what I also received, that Christ died for our sins in accordance with the scriptures, and that he was buried, that he was raised on the third day in accordance with the scriptures, and that he appeared to Cephas, then to the twelve. Then he appeared to more than five hundred brethren at one time. . . .

The Gospel which we are asked to believe concerns Jesus Christ. It consists of certain facts about His life — i.e. that He died, was buried and then rose again from the dead. To become a Christian we must accept these things to be so. In accepting these facts, we are also accepting Jesus' assessment of Himself as the Son of God, because it is by the death/resurrection event that we know this to be true.

But there is more to this statement of the Gospel than a recitation of historical facts. There are three key words of interpretation — the words *"for our sins."*

In the act of repentance we are brought face to face with our real self — the self living apart from God, living rather in sin. We are also made to realize that by ourselves we can do nothing to alter our sin-prone nature or to change our relationship with God. "We cannot straighten or heal ourselves, or create integrity in ourselves, because we have nothing to work with except our sick and disintegrated selves. And since all our fellows share that inherent disability, no other human being can do for us what we cannot do for ourselves. The physician cannot heal himself. . . ."[6] To be healed we need outside help. We need God's help. And this is precisely what we are, in fact, asked to believe — that Christ has died for sins, and in so doing dealt with our sinful natures.

There are in general three ways by which an omnipotent God could heal us. With a wave of His hand, so to speak, He could override our divided wills, minds, bodies and hearts. If He did, however, He would destroy our freedom and turn us into slaves or puppets. . . . Or God could prescribe for us a course of action, promulgate a set of rules, which when followed would result in a cure. Many people believe that this is what He has done, and all that He has done, but at best it is a partial measure because its success depends upon what man can do by means of his own efforts. . . .

Therefore, Christianity says, God took a third way in which our sin is not amputated as by surgery, or forced into line as by a brace, but is healed as by medicine. The following analogy should not be pressed too far, but it will serve my immediate purpose. As animals are inoculated with certain viruses in order to develop antibodies that can be made into vaccines, so God voluntarily contracted man's disease of sin, knowing that only He could produce antibodies that would be effective against the disease, and knowing also that the process would require Him to suffer the agony and death that result from sin. He had to be fully man so that the disease could infect Him. He had to be fully God so that He could develop antibodies for our healing. Only by receiving this vaccine could men be cured without being irremediably maimed in the process. It is as simple and as fundamental as that.[7]

Christ died for our sins to enable us to come back to God and hence to come alive. As St. Paul put it: "To you, who were spiritually dead all the time that you drifted along on the stream of this world's ideas of living, and obeyed its unseen ruler . . . to you Christ has given life! We all lived like that in the past . . . But even though we were dead in our sins God, who is rich in mercy, because of the great love He had for us, gave us life together with Christ. . . ."[8] Our sin made our spiritual natures dead. Because Christ died for our sins, we can be made alive. This is the *fundamental assertion of the Gospel which we must believe to become a Christian.*

b. How do we believe?

But how do we "believe"? What is involved in the act of belief? Certainly there is the idea of intellectual acceptance. Our mind has to say: "Yes, this is true." None of us are capable of consciously following what we consider to be a lie. But when the word "believe" is used in the New Testament, it involves more than mere assent to a set of propositions. If we "believe" in the Biblical sense, we act. Acceptance of certain assertions must issue in action if it is to be real "belief" — or "faith."

> Formal belief — intellectual conviction — becomes real belief or faith at the point when we act upon it. When, after considering evidence for and against the proposition that so-and-so is true, we come to a definite conclusion, we have reached formal belief. When our conclusion influences our further thinking and behaviour, we have faith. We not only believe it; we believe in it. We trust it enough to allow it to determine how we live. Real belief is demonstrated in a small but significant way every time we walk across a floor without thinking about what we are doing. We should behave differently if we really believed that what appeared to be a solid floor actually consisted of painted paper laid across an abyss. The Christian, having real belief in a loving God, behaves differently from the person who really believes all notions of God to be convenient but rather juvenile projections of men's current emotional states.[9]

This leads us quite directly to the third and final aspect of becoming a Christian. Once we have understood our true state of alienation from God and have decided to end our rebellion (repentance) and have come to believe that through Christ's death for our sins this is possible (faith), we are then bidden to "follow Christ." Such a step is the inevitable consequence of authentic belief. If we do really *believe*, we will follow Christ.

3. *Follow Christ*

But a man does not automatically follow Christ. He must

choose to do so. Hence "following Christ" has a beginning point. This beginning point is called conversion. It is literally the point of "turning from sin to Christ."

It is fairly plain therefore (no matter how much we dislike facing the fact) that every individual man is either following Christ or not following Christ. There is no neutral ground. This is, of course, one of the imperatives to evangelism. We look around us and we see the half-lives men are leading and we are compelled to say to them: "There is no reason to go on destroying yourself. Start following Christ. Let Him begin to remake you."

However, we must be wary of defining too precisely just what that beginning point must look like. In any study of conversion experiences, the first fact that impresses itself on one is the wide variety of responses to Christ. For some, the experience is virtually instantaneous. For others, the turning process is spread over years. For still others, there is never any conscious awareness of the process of turning — only the present consciousness of following Christ.

a. We Are Being Remade

But the beginning is not the whole story. Notice carefully our Lord's call to Simon and Andrew. "Follow me and *I will make you become fishers of men."* He is calling them to become something. He wants to make them into something. To follow Christ involves not only beginning but continuing.

The reason for this is clear. When we come to Christ, we are not automatically, instantaneously remade into little saints, full of wisdom and righteousness, perfect in all ways. That part of our nature which is sinful is not eradicated. Rather it is dethroned and taken from the center of our life and our newly alive spiritual nature becomes the focal point of our personality. But the continuing presence of our old nature signifies warfare. Becoming a Christian marks the beginning of the conflict between our old and new natures — a conflict which is finally resolved only when we meet Christ face to face at death. And only as we continue to follow

Christ can we win the battle with sin, as we allow Him, gradually and patiently to remake us. In exactly the same way as we come to Christ, via repentance and belief, we follow after Him. We grow in our understanding and trust of Jesus and what He can do in and through us (belief). We continue to change our mind about ourselves as we see ourselves ever more clearly, and we allow our behavior to change (repentance). The Christian life is a life of continuous repentance and faith.

b. We Are Following a Person

Note too that we are called upon to follow a person not a principle. "Follow *Christ*," we are told. Quite frankly, one of the problems in the Church today is misunderstanding at this point. So often, Christian commitment is conceived of as trust in a creed, loyalty to an institution, or faithfulness in devotion. While all these are involved in following Christ, they are not the following itself. To be a Christian means to be involved, on the deepest level of our being, with the person of Christ; the Savior who was resurrected and is still alive. To make Christianity less than this is to deny its essence.

This, incidentally, explains how it is possible for conversion experiences to be so different for different people. In conversion, we come to a Person *who meets us where we are.* We are not asked to become anything before we can be a Christian. We do not have to clean ourselves up, so to speak. We are asked, simply, to open ourselves, in whatever state we are, to the Living Christ who stands outside our life asking entrance.

This also explains why we then begin to grow and change when we come to Jesus. We have entered into a *relationship* with a Person, and, as in all relationships, we change in response to the ongoing demands the Other places upon us. If Christianity were mere commitment to a creed, our growth would end at the point when we were able to believe the creed. A creed is a dead thing, unable to make any other demand upon us than intellectual acceptance.

c. Following Christ Is Like Marriage

Let me try to sum this all up by describing commitment to Christ in terms of marriage, for herein we have a perfect illustration (sanctioned by Scripture) of what we are called upon to do.

> Mere intellectual assent to facts does not make a person a Christian any more than mere intellectual assent to facts makes a person married. Many people's dissatisfaction with Christianity is because they are like a person who says: "I believe in marriage, I'm sold on marriage, I've read a dozen books on marriage and in the last three months I've been to fifteen weddings, but for some strange reason marriage doesn't mean anything to me." The reason is very simple: he isn't married. Marriage is not a philosophy . . . nor is Christianity . . . rather it is a dynamic relationship with a living person, the Lord Jesus Christ. Just as getting married means giving up our independence, so does receiving Christ. The essence of sin is living independently of God — going my way rather than His way. The essence of repentance is the repudiation of the self-centred principle making Christ and His will the centre of my life. When we marry we think of another person in all our decisions. When we receive Christ, we enter into a consultative relationship with Him about every area of our lives.[10]

Continuing the marriage illustration:

> . . . when we confront Jesus our situation becomes almost identical with that of a girl who has received a proposal of marriage. The circumstances compel us to make a decision. We must move from formal belief (the girl accepts or rejects the proposal) to real belief (she marries or does not marry this man). Once the proposal has been made, an answer must be given. Once it has been spoken and heard, neither the lover's "Will you marry me?" nor Jesus' "Will you follow me?" can be evaded. As Gregory Vlastos has written: "There are a thousand ways of saying no; one way of saying yes; and no way of saying anything else." To refuse to answer is an answer. To put off answering is an answer. So is the sudden, surprised recognition that we have

already crossed the line between "no" and "yes," in either direction, without realizing at the time that the movement was implied by some other decision. And, of course, to answer forthrightly is to answer.[11]

COMMUNICATING THE GOSPEL

It has become apparent that there are three conditions which need to be fulfilled in order for a person to come to know Christ. These are summed up by the key words: *repentance; faith* (i.e. belief); and *obedience* (i.e. following Jesus). Let us now discuss how we can communicate these theological ideas in non-theological terms as we seek to introduce a friend to Jesus.

1. *Awareness of Need*

Repentance begins with an awareness of need. This awareness of need, however, comes to different people in different ways. For some it comes by way of the experience of deep loneliness. For others, the purposelessness of their life is their point of discomfort. Still others sense their need by becoming aware of their longing for "more" in this life — more peace, or more purpose, or more self-control. Some are driven by the awareness that there is no meaning in their life. Others are bewildered by a sense of guilt; or distressed by a sense of anxiety about death. In all these ways (and many more) men and women *experience the fact of sin.* This is the basis of repentance — awareness of our true situation (i.e. something really is wrong in us) and the desire to do something about it.

Sometimes the impulse to follow Christ comes not so much from dissatisfaction with the way we have been living, as from a longing to come into the new life which Christ brings. An individual discovers all the riches that Christ offers and ardently desires to possess them. It is the anticipation of what *can be* rather than a distaste for what *has been* that brings him to Christ.

But what of those individuals who seem to have no needs;

who seem perfectly satisfied with their experience of life? It must be pointed out that such people do have needs, whether or not they are aware of them (or will admit them). Any psychologist will tell you that there is no such thing as a person without inner needs and longings. People may be *unaware* of their needs because they are so out of touch with their "real self." When any "dark thoughts" emerge they are promptly pushed down and hidden away behind the mask such a person wears in public. Nevertheless, the needs are there.

What can we do to help our friends become aware of their inner need? First of all, we can be honest with them about our own "dark side." As they see us face this and admit what we are really like, they are encouraged to admit (even if only to themselves) that they too are needy people. This is the honesty principle once again.

Second, we can help them see their need by helping them see the glorious reality of Christ. St. Paul says: "All have sinned and come short of the glory of God."[12] If people can see the "glory of God" they will begin to see their own sin which keeps them from it. They see the "glory of God" when they see what Jesus can do in a life; when they see what He offers; when, in fact, they see Jesus. However, we often try to apply this verse in reverse. We say to our friends, directly or indirectly: "You are a sinner." As this is a form of judgment, their response, as Scripture tells us to anticipate,[13] is to close up and say to us: "Well, you are not so perfect yourself."

Third, we can pray for such a person that the scales will drop from his eyes so that he can "see" Christ and "see" himself as he really is.

Once there is awareness of need, our aim is to help our friend *identify* what this inner sense of need really is, i.e. a sign of his separation from God. "You feel lonely because you were made to know God." Or, "Your sense of guilt comes because ultimately only God can forgive us." Or, "The fear of death can only be overcome through the hope of the resurrection that God's children have." Or, "Peace comes as a by-product of the sense of God's presence." In essence we *interpret* for our friend the real meaning of his inner longing.

But an awareness of need is not enough. There must also be a desire to do something about this need. There must be a longing to put behind the old, self-oriented style of life and begin a new life in Christ. There must be the willingness to leave our sin. There must be an awareness that we need forgiveness. Repentance is a "turning from sin *to Christ.*"

2. *Faith in Christ*

This brings us to the second step in coming to Christ: belief that one can be forgiven; can leave the old behind; and can begin a new life in Christ. Coupled with an understanding of need must also be the awareness that because Christ died, one can be forgiven for the past and come into the relationship with God that is longed for. Our job is to communicate this fact to our friend. "Christ died for our sins . . . that He might bring us to God." This will involve us in a discussion of who Jesus is and what He has done. When a friend believes that through Christ's death he can come to know Christ, he is ready to follow Christ. In fact, his obedience in following Christ is proof of his belief.

3. *Obedience in Following*

Repentance and faith must then be completed by means of an act of commitment whereby the person consciously gives himself to Christ to be His follower.

This act of commitment can be described in terms of Revelation 3:20 in which Christ is pictured as standing outside a life, asking to come in as Lord and Master. The response to Him must be as definite an act as reaching out and grasping a door handle and then opening that door. Or, the response can be described as an act as definite as saying "yes" in a marriage ceremony and hence entering into a lifelong relationship with another person.

Such an act of commitment can take place anywhere and any time. C. S. Lewis was riding atop a bus when he first opened himself to God. Others have been sitting in a church, or standing amongst enquirers at an evangelistic meeting. John Stott, one of the Queen's Chaplains in England, knelt at his bedside one Sunday night in the dormitory of his public school and told Christ that he had made rather a mess of his life so far; he confessed his sins; he thanked Christ for dying for him; and he asked Him to come into his life. The following day he wrote in his diary: "Yesterday really *was* an eventful day! . . . Up till now Christ has been on the circumference and I have but asked Him to guide me instead of giving Him complete control. Behold! He stands at the door and knocks. I have heard Him and now is He come into my house. He has cleansed it and now rules there-in . . . !"[14]

Your friend may well want your guidance when he comes to this point of commitment. Here is a prayer he can follow:

Lord Jesus, I realize that thus far I have been living my life apart from You, motivated almost solely by what I wanted. I am really sorry for the way in which I have sinned in thought, word and deed. I now turn from this self-centered life as best I can, and pledge by Your grace, to lead a new life with You as my Master.

I believe that this is possible because You died on the Cross for my sins. Thank You for what You have done.

And now I come to You and commit myself to You. Make of me what You will. I am Yours Lord Jesus from this day forward.

Amen

THE USE OF THE STATEMENT

Let me conclude with some comments about the use to which one can put such an outline of the gospel message. Quite simply, this formulation (repentance, faith and obedience) and others like it, are intended to aid you in introducing your friends to Jesus. This is, of course, the ultimate aim of all witness: to see one's friends discover the power and reality of the living Christ. And in order for them to do this, it is our responsibility to provide them with the data necessary to make a real decision. Before a man can honestly evaluate Christianity he must have something to evaluate. Hence the attempt to formulate concisely the essence of Christian commitment.

Of course, in trying to do this, we are doomed to failure. For one thing, Christianity is all about commitment to a Person, not to a set of propositions — which is what any formulation is. Hence any set of propositions will be incomplete.

Furthermore, it is true that many people have become genuine Christians without even this minimal *conceptual* understanding of the Gospel. Some are merely aware of Christ — and they are irresistibly drawn to Him, although they seem to have little consciousness of sin. Others, in great need, quite literally cast themselves upon God's mercy, with only a vague awareness of Jesus. When I became a Christian as a child, as best I can remember, my only reaction to the Cross was a feeling of anger that bad men did this to Jesus who certainly did not deserve to die.

The point is this: in Christian commitment we come to a Person, Jesus. What is key is our sense of Him, not the depth of our doctrinal understanding.

Yet, if a man has in fact met Christ, he will grow in his understanding of what took place and why. In my own case, I began to learn about the meaning of the Cross when I joined a church while in high school. Yet it was only in theological seminary that I really came to grips with the wonder of the atonement.

This growth in understanding is essential. It is one of the marks of the genuineness of the conversion experience.

In all this, we dare not forget that it is, ultimately, God who saves us. The validity of commitment to Christ does not depend on the depth of our understanding but upon the inner work of the Holy Spirit.

After all this you might well ask: "But what then is the value of an outline such as has been presented here?" First of all, it is valuable for us as Christians in that it provides a framework around which to build up our own theological understanding. So many Christians have difficulty in putting into words their experience of Christ because they have no such outline to serve as the structure for their thoughts. Once you have memorized such an outline, you can begin to fill it out by reading (see the bibliography at the end of the chapter) and by conversation as well as by Bible study.

Then too, once you have grasped such a formulation of the Gospel you will have a sense of security and direction as you talk with non-Christians. You will know what you want to say and what direction a conversation must take as you seek to introduce someone to Jesus.

However, any formulation must be held lightly. As Paul Little has written:

> Because the Gospel is about a person, there is no rigid and rote way in which it is to be presented. Whenever we are talking about a person rather than a formula, we always begin with the aspect of a person's appearance, character and personality that is most relevant at the moment. If you have a blond brother who is studying at Harvard, you don't begin the conversation by saying: "I have a brother who is blond, is studying chemistry, and is at Harvard." Rather, you begin, "Oh, I have a brother who is at Harvard," and you may then go to the other facts as they are relevant. On the other hand if you meet someone who is almost an identical twin to your brother, you wouldn't begin by saying that you have a brother who is studying chemistry. Rather you might say, "You look just like my brother," and then go on to other facts.
>
> In the same way, when we are talking about the Lord Jesus Christ, it may be that at one time His resurrection is the most relevant aspect of His person and work. Another time it might be His death, another His diagnosis of human nature, and another time who He is. Eventually, we want to cover all the information in the Gospel. We must be conversant with the basic facts about the Lord Jesus Christ that a person ought to know to become a Christian[15]

The Content of Witness (Part 2)

A Dialogue About Commitment

There are certain passages in Scripture which are particularly valuable to have at your finger tips in any witness situation because they communicate key ideas so concisely (and often so beautifully). Below are some such verses which relate to the outline given in the text of the lecture. Why not memorize these verses?[16]

1. *Repentance*

   (a) "All have sinned and fall short of the glory of God" (Romans 3:23).

   (b) "For the wages of sin is death, but the free gift of God is eternal life in Christ Jesus our Lord" (Romans 6:23).

2. *Faith*

   (a) "For Christ died for sins, once for all, the righteous for the unrighteous that He might bring us to God" (I Peter 3:18).

   (b) "For God so loved the world that He gave His only Son, that whoever believes in Him should not perish but have eternal life. For God sent the Son into the world, not to condemn the world, but that the world might be saved through Him" (John 3:16, 17).

3. *Obedience*

   (a) "Behold, I stand at the door and knock; if any one hears my voice and opens the door, I will come into him and eat with him, and he with me" (Revelation 3:20).

   (b) "But to all who received him (Christ), who believed in His name, He gave power to become the children of God" (John 1:12).

Now continue the dialogue you began last week. Try to explain to your interested non-Christian friend how he can actually become a Christian. Try to include some of the memorized verses in your dialogue.

1. *Continue sharing* about Christ with your friends. Share, in particular, with at least one other person your own experience of Jesus.

2. *Continue praying* for such opportunities as well as for your friends.

3. *Practice explaining how to become a Christian* by means of an inner dialogue. By this I mean, try to imagine discussing Christ with a friend. What would he say? How would you respond? Actually this is a very valuable method of practice. It helps you think through issues without consuming much time.

The Content of Witness (Part 2)

The Art of Introduction

By Bruce Larson

Jesus Christ is a living person; not a theory, nor a law, nor a theological truth. Theology is important for a more complete understanding of Christ, but the Christian life begins when we are introduced to *the* Friend. It is that simple.

Nothing is more needed today in the Church than introducers. When you know Christ as a person, you can introduce Him to another and trust that He will be eager to reveal Himself.

There is freedom if we realize that proper titles and definitive terms about Christ are unnecessary in the art of introduction. A scientist friend of mine tells about one of his colleagues who was intrigued by the Christian life through contact with a lunch-hour group meeting in his lab. After many months he came to my friend and said he wanted to find the kind of life he had seen in this small group of men. "I know that commitment is the answer," he announced, "but I don't believe in God, let alone Jesus Christ, so how can I find what you have found?"

"Tell me, can you make a turnip?" my friend asked, remembering something he had heard elsewhere.

"Of course not."

"Do you know of anyone who can make a turnip?"

"No."

"Well, will you turn your life over to the person who makes turnips?"

The man did exactly that. And then Jesus Christ — the author and creator of all things, the "turnip maker" — began to reveal Himself. Through joining the group and reading the Bible regularly the man in a short time acquired much biblical and doctrinal knowledge, but this knowledge about Christ came *after* the introduction.

The Church today is like a corporation with a marvelous advertising campaign but very few salesmen in the field. An ever-increasing number of people have discovered Life and can witness compellingly, humorously, and effectively about Christ. But where are the introducers?

It is high adventure to stand by while a person meets the Person and begins a new style of life. Here are three suggestions which may prove helpful in acquiring the art of introduction:

First, new life can start when a person begins a relationship with Jesus Christ in which, for him, there are no conscious reservations. Our job is not to anticipate the things in someone's life which may need to be dealt with, but to suggest that he give Christ all he sees at the moment.

Second, suggest that this commitment to Christ be as specific as possible.

Third, encourage your friend to make this commitment aloud in your presence — even as marriage vows are exchanged in the presence of witnesses.

One of the most effective Christians I know is a garage owner on Long Island. Though he was a church member, Al resisted turning his life over to "new management." Then one night, after a long conversation with a friend who was a newspaper editor in a nearby town, the editor said: "Well, Al, if you are satisfied with your life the way it is, forget about this commitment to Christ."

Al was troubled for days. He had many doctrinal questions about the person of Christ and the necessity for commitment, but he was not satisfied with his life. Some days later he returned to his editor friend, and met Jesus Christ as his Lord.

Recently I met a skeptical young man who had just been discharged from the Marine Corps. George seemed so negative about everything Christian that it surprised me when he confided that he was secretly reading many books about Christ, but was not convinced.

"I want to know if Jesus Christ is real," he said. "If He is, I want to give Him my life. If not, I want to forget all about this stuff."

I suggested an experiment: that if there really was someone called Christ who loved George and was eager to give him new life, He could make Himself known in many convincing ways. But if there was no such person, the experiment would make that obvious.

"I'll buy that," he answered. We bowed our heads and after a long pause George said something like this: "Jesus, I don't know if You are real, but if You are and if You can hear me and if You care for me, I turn my life over to You unreservedly."

When George looked up there were tears in his eyes, and he said: "I hope He is real."

After a bit, I asked: "How will you know if your life has been changed? You can't depend on feelings, because they come and go. What are some things that will be different if Christ has taken charge?"

He thought for a minute and mentioned several obvious things that would be typical of most young men. Then he said: "I will *really* know that I am different if I can love my dad when I drive home from the factory tomorrow. Every day he lectures me on how I should work harder, apply myself more, and not be a failure. He means well, but his sermons bug me, and I sit there seething with resentment."

Later in the week a letter came telling of a whole new relationship between the young man and his father. Christ revealed Himself to George in a way he could understand.

The Long Island editor was very wise when he stopped arguing doctrine with the garage owner and said: "Are you satisfied with your life the way it is?" This is a much more effective approach than trying to convince a skeptic that Jesus was born of a virgin, walked on water, turned water into wine, and all the rest.

There are many questions that God will give us at the right moment to move the issue from the doctrinal to the volitional. One such question is: "What do you want to do with your life?" Someone has said: "More people are kept from the Kingdom of God by cold feet than by cold logic."

As with George, the Marine, it is helpful to get people to express the specific things in their lives which they know are wrong and which need to be changed. This is how we affirm that Jesus Christ is the Evangelist, and that He has spoken to the person long before we entered the picture. The skillful introducer will give the other person a chance to report those things and to nail them down.

There is no fixed pattern or sequence in the art of introduction. Once a man drove 200 miles to see me for the express purpose of giving his life to Christ. For two hours we sat in my study while I asked him to tell me the things in his life that needed changing, but he kept insisting, "I can't think of a thing."

I probed and probed until I almost killed the patient. Finally I asked: "Well, why don't we get on with the business of commitment?" "That's what I came for," he replied. As we knelt together, this man made a stumbling but genuine surrender — and *then* for the next half hour he poured out the habits, fears, sins and wrong relationships of a lifetime.

D. T. Niles says that evangelism is simply one beggar telling another where to find bread. If in introducing, we realize we are not teaching great doctrinal truths, the issue becomes relatively simple. It is simple because Christ Himself is the Evangelist, and we merely cooperate with Him.

We must seek spiritual skills as earnestly as we seek social skills. But the important thing is to begin now to be introducers. Introducing others to Christ is normal Christianity. The fun begins when we start to practice the art of introduction.*

*From *Setting Men Free* (Grand Rapids: Zondervan Publishing House, 1967), pp. 37-41.

Bibliography

1. *How to Become a Christian* by Samuel Shoemaker; Harper and Row.
2. *The Open Heart* by Rosalind Rinker; Zondervan.
3. *Becoming a Christian* by John Stott; IVF Booklet.
4. *What Makes a Man a Christian?* by Timothy Dudley-Smith; Hodder and Stoughton.
*5. *Invitation to Pilgrimage* by John Baille; Pelican Book.
6. *Basic Christianity* by John Stott. See especially Chapters 9 and 10.
*7. *A Creed for a Christian Skeptic* by Mary McDermott Shideler; Eerdmans.

Chapter 8

The Strategy of Witness

The Strategy of Witness

Group Exercises

PHASE I: *The Lecture* (15 minutes)

In this final session we are shifting our usual format and beginning with the lecture. Also, rather than a recorded lecture, the group leader himself will summarize chapter eight. Sit back now and listen. Take notes on what to remember when you set about planning your own outreach group.

PHASE II: *Planning Outreach Groups* (50 minutes)

Now it is up to you to plan your outreach groups. You will have to come to decisions in the following areas:

1. *Splitting Up*: How will your training group split up into various outreach groups?

2. *Targets*: What is the target for each group? How will you invite people? Will you do visitation?

3. *Venue*:

4. *Type of Group*:

5. *Length*:

6. *Content*: What materials will you use?

7. *Future Planning*: Plan the next meeting for each of the newly formed outreach groups in which to do specific planning of your program. In addition do you want to meet all together once more as a fellowship group before outreach begins?

PHASE III: *Worship Together* (20 minutes)

What better way to end your group training experience than by a time of prayer, sharing, and worship together?

1. *Hymns*: Begin by singing (or reading) a hymn together. Below are several to choose from:

(a) *Guide me, O Thou great Jehovah,*
Pilgrim through this barren land;

I am weak, but Thou art mighty,
Hold me with Thy powerful hand;
Bread of heaven,
Feed me till I want no more.

Open now the crystal fountain
Whence the healing stream doth flow;
Let the fire and cloudy pillar
Lead me all my journey through;
Strong Deliverer,
Be Thou still my strength and shield.

When I tread the verge of Jordan,
Bid my anxious fears subside;
Death of death, and hell's Destruction,
Land me safe on Canaan's side;
Songs of praises
I will ever give to Thee.

(b) *Praise, my soul, the King of heaven,*
To His feet thy tribute bring;
Ransomed, healed, restored, forgiven,
Who like thee His praise should sing?
Praise Him! Praise Him!
Praise the everlasting King.

Praise Him for His grace and favor
To our fathers in distress;
Praise Him, still the same for ever,
Slow to chide and swift to bless;
Praise Him! Praise Him!
Glorious in His faithfulness.

2. *Prayers*: Praise God for who He is, what He has done and what He will do. Begin by praying together the prayer below, which is one of the ancient prayers of the Church. Then carry on, praying spontaneously. Remember to pray simply, in sentences, specifically, and in the first person.

Almighty God, Father of all mercies, we thine un-
worthy servants, do give thee most humble and
hearty thanks for all thy goodness and loving-kind-
ness to us, and to all men; We bless thee for our
creation, preservation, and all the blessings of this
life; but above all, for thine inestimable love in the
redemption of the world by our Lord Jesus Christ;
for the means of grace, and for the hope of glory.
And, we beseech thee, give us that due sense of
all thy mercies, that our hearts may be unfeignedly
thankful; and that we show forth thy praise, not
only with our lips, but in our lives, by giving up our
selves to thy service, and by walking before thee in
holiness and righteousness all our days; through Jesus Christ our Lord, to whom, with thee and the
Holy Ghost be all honour and glory, world without
end.

Amen.

Book of Common Prayer

3. *Sharing*: Spend the next few moments sharing together. As preparation for this, think silently about
what you might share with the group from your experience in the past weeks. What has been especially
meaningful to you? What has been hard for you?
What was the high point of the group? What is your
anticipation for the future? If you share aloud with
the group, remember to do so briefly.

4. *Prayer for the Future*: Pray together again, now focus-
sing your prayer on what lies ahead.

5. *Hymns*: End with a hymn. Below are some more to
choose from:

(a) *Crown Him with many crowns,*
     The Lamb upon His throne:
     Hark how the heavenly anthem drowns
     All music but its own.
     Awake my soul, and sing

Of Him who died for thee,
And hail Him as thy matchless King
Through all eternity.

Crown Him the Lord of life,
Who triumphed o'er the grave,
And rose victorious in the strife
For those He came to save.
His glories now we sing
Who died and rose on high,
Who died eternal life to bring,
And lives that death may die.

Crown Him the Lord of Love;
Behold His hands and side,
Those wounds yet visible above,
In beauty glorified.
All hail, Redeemer, hail!
For thou hast died for me:
Thy praise shall never, never fail
Throughout eternity.

(b)   *Join all the glorious names*
Of wisdom, love, and power,
That ever mortals knew,
That angels ever bore;
All are too mean to speak His worth,
Too mean to set my Saviour forth.

Great Prophet of my God,
My tongue would bless Thy name;
By Thee the joyful news
Of our salvation came;
The joyful news of sins forgiven,
Of hell subdued, and peace with heaven.

(c)   *Now thank we all our God,*
With hearts and hands and voices,
Who wondrous things hath done,
In whom His world rejoices,
Who, from our mother's arms,

Hath blessed us on our way
With countless gifts of love,
And still is ours today.

O may this bounteous God
Through all our life be near us,
With ever-joyful hearts
And blessed peace to cheer us,
And keep us in His grace,
And guide us when perplexed,
And free us from all ills
In this world and the next.

All praise and thanks to God
The Father now be given,
The Son, and Him who reigns
With them in highest heaven,
The one, eternal God,
Whom earth and heaven adore;
For thus it was, is now,
And shall be evermore.

Study Schedule

READ:

1. *The Text of the Lecture.*
2. *Sections from those books in the Bibliography* which deal with aspects of this lecture which especially puzzle or interest you. In particular, note those books and booklets which can aid you in your witness.

CONSIDER FOR YOURSELF:

"What Is Next?" as a review of what you learned and experienced and as a plan for the future.

ACT:

1. *By considering* past lessons.
2. *By planning* for the future.

A Strategy for Outreach

"Perhaps the time is ripe for co-ordinating mass evangelism with the development of small, disciplined groups or cells that regularly meet to share, study, pray and witness."[1]

Leighton Ford

In past chapters it has been the constant assertion that "by means of small groups one can do evangelism in an exciting and profitable way." Now it is time to examine just how groups can be used in this way.

AN OVERALL PLAN

To be of real value, a training group (such as you have been part of for these past weeks) must develop into an outreach group. Your whole preparation has been with this end in mind.

You will remember from the Introduction that it was suggested that the training group be used as the first phase in an evangelistic program; followed by outreach groups, a series of preaching meetings (if the evangelistic endeavor is part of a total church program); and then follow-up Bible study groups.

This plan will be too ambitious for some groups. However, at least the second phase ought to be entered into by every training group. *For the training to have been meaningful, outreach groups should be formed.*

This can be done by splitting up the present training group. For example, imagine a hypothetical training group of say twelve. From this, three outreach groups could be formed. Let us say that two couples live near one another, so they decide to form a home evangelism group to which they will invite their friends and neighbors. Three of the group members are businessmen working in the same area of the city. They decide to create a lunch-time outreach group for their colleagues. The remaining five people form themselves into a second home evangelism unit, meeting where the training group met.

Note what has happened. Twelve Christians have met together for eight weeks to receive training in outreach. Now, rather than staying together to enjoy the continued fellowship (and this will be a *very* strong temptation, especially if you grew to know and love one another during the group sessions), they split up into three outreach groups. The potential of such multiplication is quite staggering. This training and splitting principle is, in fact, the key to evangelism.

RECRUITING FOR GROUPS

Once groups are formed around a nucleus of Christians, how are new people added?

The easiest and most natural way of doing this is by issuing personal invitations to friends. You have already had experience in doing this — both in recruiting for the training group and in inviting your friends to the Outreach Evening. But let us think some more about the art of invitation.

The best way to issue an invitation is face to face. In this way you are best able to convey your own sense of excitement about the group, and thus you can arouse your friend's interest.

Even though it is best, it is not always possible to see a friend personally, so here is where the telephone comes in. A telephone is a marvelous device. It takes little time to use and it reaches out even to our most elusive friends. And once a person is on the telephone, dialogue is guaranteed.

In some situations, a letter or card is the appropriate means of invitation. They are best used as a follow-up to a personal invitation, however.

In inviting people, it is most important to be honest with them. They must know exactly what they are invited to attend. Whatever you do, do not trap friends into an outreach group when they are expecting just the usual dinner-party. This will not only be embarrassing to you, but it could be harmful.

For example, some years ago an energetic group of Christians on one university campus planned a special banquet for athletes. They issued invitations to all the campus athletes, prepared an excellent dinner, and invited in nationally known sports figures as speakers. The only thing they forgot to do was to mention that the banquet was sponsored by the Christian group on the campus and that the well-known sports figures were all Christians and would be speaking primarily about their faith and not about their sports exploits. A large group of athletes came to the banquet — and when they discovered what they were attending, their overwhelming feeling was that of having been tricked. After the banquet, protests were made to university officials, who in turn banned further campus activities of this Christian group. Far from helping evangelism on the campus, the ministry of this group was hindered for years to come.

So be honest. Tell your friends what is planned and why. Tell them that the aim of the group is to provoke discussion about Christianity — and in particular its relevance to individuals living in this day and age. Tell them what will happen during the evening.

Invite them to the first session, indicating that a total of four to six weekly meetings are planned (or however many you may decide upon), but that if after the first meeting they do not feel that this is the sort of thing they enjoy, they are under no obligation to carry on.

In some situations you may feel that it would be best to invite people to one session only — and then, if it goes well, inquire then and there if they would like to carry on for some more sessions.

Be honest and natural in your invitation. Remember that what you are offering to people is a unique opportunity: the chance to get together on an informal basis with like-minded men and women to hear an excellent tape (or see a film, or study a book, etc.) and then to discuss in a low-pressure way the implications of Christianity. Most people would jump at such a chance. Never forget that people *do* want to discuss Christianity.

Be careful, however, not to invite too many. Eight to twelve is a good number for a group. You can anticipate that 70-80 percent of your invitations will be accepted. How many you invite relates to the number of committed Christians in the group. At least 30 percent of the group should be Christians, but not more than 50 percent.

A second way in which to contact people for the group is by means of visiting homes in the neighborhood. This is not an unfamiliar method to many Christians, since churches quite often conduct what are called "Visitation Campaigns." The advantage of such a visiting program is that people are reached who probably otherwise would have no contact with a church.

If your group decides to visit in the neighborhood I would suggest the following:

1. Set aside an appropriate time in which to visit. This will depend upon the Target group. If your aim is to start a morning group for housewives, visit in the morning. Be sure to pick a time when people are likely to be in and not rushed.

2. Meet as a group beforehand to discuss where you are going to visit and to pray together. Do not take too much time on this, however, lest you have no time left for visiting!

3. Go out in pairs to visit the predetermined area. At each home:
   (a) Introduce yourself clearly, and say why you have come ("to invite you to a meeting in a nearby home").
   (b) Chat for a few minutes.
   (c) Leave behind a written (or printed) invitation giving all the details.
   (d) If they are interested in coming, see if you can help in terms of transportation, baby-sitters, etc.

One more note: for an invitation to be effective, it ought to begin in prayer. Ask God to prepare your friends to receive your invitation graciously and to accept it. Pray then

221

that He will prepare them to hear the Gospel with real understanding. Pray for yourself, that you will be able to issue the invitation with real love and sensitivity.

CONTENT OF THE GROUPS

Now that you have your group together, what are you going to do? This is a decision which your group must make. As a guide for you, a number of possible group programs were discussed in Chapter 4. More programs are outlined in the Group Leader's Manual.

In addition it might be good to assign one or two group members to survey materials which could be used at an outreach meeting. Get catalogs from the Christian film libraries in the area. There are an increasing number of tape libraries which stock suitable materials which can be ordered by letter. For example, The Electric Message (P.O. Box 4728, Santa Barbara, Calif. 93103) has excellent tapes for young people. Records of first rate sermons and lectures are also available in stores.

CONTINUATION OF GROUPS

Thus far we have discussed two types of groups: training groups (in which you have been involved) and outreach groups (which you are planning). A third type is the follow-up group,[2] the aim of which is to discuss by means of Bible study what it means to live like a Christian.

Some groups may well want to continue even after these follow-up Bible studies. In the Bibliography, I have listed materials which you can obtain in order to carry on. Groups can be especially valuable as a spearhead for service in the community.

LITERATURE AND GROUPS

Once you have decided on the content of your group, give some thought to literature which could be taken home by everyone after each session which would complement and draw together the discussion of the evening. Many good books and booklets are readily available.

Actually, literature is a very valuable aid in your witness, not only on a group level, but individually.

1. *Booklets*

Booklets are especially valuable for very busy people, because they are short enough to be read in one sitting, but long enough to say something with a bit of depth.

I once gave a friend of mine *Have You Considered Him?* (a booklet about the person of Jesus). He took it home and actually read it, though, as he later confessed, he does not usually read much. He started to read this booklet because it seemed brief enough to get through. He kept on reading it because it was so fascinating. You should keep on hand a small stock of such booklets to give to your friends.

2. *Books*

Other people, however, are willing to read a book, especially if what it discusses is a live issue with them. There are many excellent books available today, often in paperback so they are inexpensive enough to buy. You really owe it to yourself to get to know the writings of men like C. S. Lewis, John Stott, J. B. Phillips, Michael Green, Bruce Larson, and John Baillie, just to mention a few who have written about theological subjects in a readable and highly interesting fashion.

Do not neglect Christian fiction in your consideration of books to share with friends. C. S. Lewis, for example, has written a superb trilogy of science-fiction stories from a Christian point of view. Charles Williams has written what can best be described as "supernatural thrillers." It is usually easier to get a friend to read a story rather than an essay.

Do not neglect the Bible when you loan books. It is surprising how few people, in this age of high literacy, have actually *read* the Bible. One reason is that in many people's minds the Bible means the King James Version with all its "thees" and "thous" and other strange words. The Bible is therefore thought of as a difficult book to understand.

But this is just not true — if one has a modern translation, and begins with the gospel accounts.

Nowadays there are plentiful, inexpensive, highly readable translations of Scripture available. Take for example, *One Way*, which is simply St. John's Gospel in J. B. Phillips' translation, illustrated with photographs of modern situations. A friend would be eager to read this.

I once gave a copy of "Good News for Modern Man" (Today's English Version of the New Testament) to a friend. He started reading casually one night before bed and became so fascinated that he kept on reading. His wife then picked it up a few days later and also became engrossed — so that they had to argue over who got the Bible to read!

There is an inherent power in Scripture. I recall a discussion once with one of the pioneer missionaries in Egypt. He said that their first approach to evangelism in Egypt was by means of disputation. They sought to engage Muslim religious leaders in public debate. This missionary said that they often won these debates (some of the early missionaries in Egypt were superbly trained men), but they never won any converts. It was only after they gave up disputation and concentrated on Bible translation and distribution, that converts came — almost always as a result of reading Scripture.

One note though about using books in your witness: it is better to loan a book to a friend than to give it to him outright. If you loan it he has to read it and return it. When he returns it, you can discuss it together.

Magazines and leaflets are also useful in witness. The key in using them (as well as with books and booklets) is to match the material to the needs and taste of the individual. Literature which can be used in this way is listed in the bibliography for this chapter.

CONCLUSION

The training course is now at an end. It is hoped that it has been a rich experience for you on many levels; and that it has provided adequate training to enable you to begin sharing the good news about Jesus with your friends; on both an individual and a group level.

As you ponder putting this training into practice it is well to recall what H. R. Weber said in chapter one about the early Christians: "One of the clues to the spontaneous mission of the ancient Church was the *strong consciousness* (on the part of each Christian) *of being God's own peculiar people.*"[3] Herein lies the secret to our motivation: an awareness of our calling to be God's persons in this world; to be the salt of the world and the light in a darkened age. As St. Peter put it: "You are a chosen race, a royal priesthood, a holy nation, *God's own people,* that you may declare the wonderful deeds of him who called you out of darkness into his marvellous light."[4]

At the same time we must avoid being overwhelmed by what Douglas Hyde has called a "minority complex."

From the time I joined the Communist Party, practically to the time when 24 years later I left it, I was conscious of the fact that our members firmly believed that, relatively few though they might be, they had a world to win and were going to win it. I came to the Catholic Church prepared for most of what I found — and it would be sheer hypocrisy to pretend that I either expected or found everything to be good. But one thing I had not bargained for was the many people I met who told me that the Catholic community in Britain suffered from something they described as a minority complex. I had not expected this, because I was coming from an organization which at that time had some 45,000 members to one which was numerically 100 times as strong and which represented some 10 percent of Britain's population.

Even in the days when we Communists could only boast some 15,000 members, we believed that when the right circumstances came, as come they must, we would make Britain Communist and would do so with the support of the mass of the people. Whatever else we may have suffered from, we had no minority complex.

Coming straight, as it were, from one world to another,

it astounded me that there should be people with such numbers at their disposal, and with the truth on their side, going around weighed down by the thought that they were a small beleaguered minority carrying on some sort of an impossible fight against a big majority. The very concept was wrong. Psychologically it was calamitous. And there was nothing in the facts, so far as I could see, to warrant such an approach.[5]

Let us flee from this "minority complex," simply because it is a lie. We are not "a beleaguered minority carrying on . . . an impossible fight." We are God's own people, followers of the risen Christ — the Christ who has defeated all powers.[6] Even though it may "appear" that evil rules on this earth now, the "reality" is that Christ reigns. And one day, in the fullness of time, that reign will be known to all. As it is now, we as Christians are called upon to spearhead the spread of the Kingdom of God here on earth. Let us joyfully accept this calling, as we trust in the reality of Christ's presence and power.

Rest on our Lord's words to you: "You did not choose me but I chose you and appointed you that you should go and bear fruit."[7]

What Is Next?

This exercise has two purposes: to serve as a review of the past and to stimulate planning for the future. Both are essential parts of strategy. Both are necessary if you are, in fact, going to translate your convictions into action. Both are necessary if this course is to be of any real value to you in a practical way.

1. What are the major lessons you have learned in these eight weeks?

2. How have you begun to put these ideas into practice?

3. What are your plans for the future?

4. What ideas are still unclear to you?

5. What can you do to gain further insight?

6. What does the phrase "to witness is to be honest" now mean to you? In what ways have you become a more honest person?

7. Who have you been praying for and what has happened so far? What must you continue to pray about?

8. Have you become friends with more non-Christians in the past weeks?

9. What have your attempts at verbal witness been like? What has or has not happened?

10. What friends can you invite to the outreach group?

11. What can you do in a practical way to ensure they are able to attend?

12. How have you become newly *aware* of opportunities for witness — by word and by deed?

13. Could you carry on an intelligent conversation about who Jesus is and how a man can know Him?

14. If not, what are your plans for developing this art?

15. Most important of all, is Jesus a reality to you now?

Action

1. *Consider* carefully the past; what you have learned and what it all means.

2. *Plan* for the future; where you are going and how to get there.

3. *Plan* for the outreach groups; who to invite, how, and when. Plan to fulfill your responsibility towards the group.

Bibliography

A. BOOKS THAT WITNESS

**1. *Mere Christianity; Miracles; The Screwtape Letters; Surprised by Joy* by C. S. Lewis; Fontana Books.

2. *Plain Christianity; God Our Contemporary; New Testament Christianity;* and *Your God Is Too Small* by J. B. Phillips; Fontana Books.

3. *The Meaning of Persons, Guilt and Grace; Escape From Loneliness* by Paul Tournier; SCM Press.

4. *Find Out for Yourself* (for teenagers) and *What Is God Like* by Eugenia Price; Zondervan.

5. *Choose Freedom; Runaway World* and *Man Alive* by Michael Green; IVF Press.

6. *The God Who Is There; Escape From Reason* and *Death in the City* by Francis Schaeffer; IVF Press.

7. *How to Become a Christian* and *The Experiment of Faith* by Samuel Shoemaker; Harper and Row.

8. *The Cross and the Switchblade* by David Wilkerson; Pyramid Books. The point of this book is: God is still alive and at work in the lives of even hardened teenage gang members.

9. *Peace with God* by Billy Graham; Pocket Books, Inc.

10. *Man's Need and God's Action* by Reuel Howe; Seabury Press.

B. BOOKLETS THAT WITNESS

1. *"Think Through" Series* by David Winter; Falcon. For example: "Can I believe in Jesus Christ."

2. Inter-Varsity Series. For example: *The Brink of Decision* by Michael Green and *The Danger of Disbelief* by Paul White.

C. GROUP MATERIALS

**1. *Groups in Action; Growth by Groups* and *Dialogue* by Lyman Coleman, The Halfway House. Some of the best material available today for use in groups.

2. *Acts Alive; The Coffee House Itch; Kaleidoscope* and *Man Alive* by Lyman Coleman; The Halfway House. Material designed for teenage groups.

3. *Conversations with Jesus; Examine the Record — Gospel of Mark; Four Men of God* by Marilyn Kunz and Catherine Schell; Neighborhood Bible Studies (P.O. Box 22, Dobbs Ferry, New York). Bible study material designed for adult discussion groups.

4. *The Character and Work of Jesus Christ* by Paul D. Steeves; *Discovering the Gospel of Mark* by Jane Hollingsworth; and *Patterns for Living with God* by Marilyn Kunz; Inter-Varsity Press. Adult Bible Study material, particularly suited for University students.

5. *Learning to Love God; Learning to Love Ourselves; Learning to Love People* by Richard Peace; Zondervan. A set of 15 Bible Studies on the theme of basic Christian living. Useful for follow-up groups.

6. *Who Is This Man?* by Rosalind Rinker; Zondervan. Bible Studies from the Book of Mark on the life of Christ, with excellent guidance for leaders as well as materials to use in the group.

Appendix A

What Non-Christians Ask

By Paul E. Little

I can predict with 95 percent accuracy the questions that will be asked me in the course of an hour's discussion with non-Christians.

These questions turn up again and again in discussions in residence halls. Christians can anticipate them and search out their answers. As we do this, the Holy Spirit will liberate us from the fear that has paralysed so many of us in the past, and make us increasingly helpful to our friends.

THE HEATHEN

The first, most common question is: "What about the heathen who have never heard of Jesus Christ? Will they be condemned to hell?"

We must begin by acknowledging that we don't know fully how God will deal with these people. Certain things are known only to God; we must concern ourselves with what He has revealed (Deuteronomy 29:29). And God has clearly revealed that He is just. On the basis of the evidence we have, we can confidently rest in His character, and trust that what He does with those who have never heard of Jesus Christ will be right.

Second, the Bible seems to indicate that if a person really seeks God, he will find God (Jeremiah 29:13). Missionary history reveals instances of missionaries led by the Holy Spirit to villages where people had been worshiping an unknown God, having realized that idols were worthless because they were the creation of their own hands. When they heard about the Living God in Jesus Christ, they immediately responded and recognized that this was the God whom they had been seeking. Man has enough basic information from the creation around him to warrant such a search if he is interested (Romans 1:20).

233

Third, it's important to realize that a person who hasn't heard of Jesus Christ will not be condemned for rejecting One about whom he has never heard. Rather his condemnation rests on his failure to measure up to his own moral standard, however high or low it may be. The assumption frequently behind the question of the heathen is that there are people in some foreign place living beautiful moral lives, whose only problem is that they have never heard of Jesus Christ. Actually, no culture exists in which the inhabitants claim to have lived up to their own standard perfectly. Every culture has a basic moral code which men knowingly violate, thereby condemning themselves (Romans 2:14, 15).

A full discussion of this question of an inherent universal moral law is found in *Mere Christianity* by C. S. Lewis.

THE SINCERE BUDDHIST

Closely related to the first question is: "What about the sincere Moslem, Buddhist, Hindu, etc? Doesn't he worship the same God, but under a different name?" In other words, "Is Jesus Christ the only way to God?"

The first thing to be seen in this question is that sincerity doesn't create truth. The basic consideration is the validity of the object in which faith or sincerity is placed. If the object of faith is invalid, all the sincerity in the world cannot change the fact that one merely has superstition. A bushman's sincere confidence in a potion given him by the village witch doctor to cure his daughter does not raise his faith beyond superstition, no matter how intense it may be. In fact, it may kill his daughter if it is not based on sound medical principles. So we must ask about the faith itself: "Is its object valid?"

Islam denies the deity of Christ. Christianity affirms it. Both cannot be true. The question is: "What is truth?"

Christians do not say that Jesus Christ is the only way to God because they have got together as a club and decided that this is true. Rather it is because Jesus Christ Himself said it, and truthfulness is inherent in His whole being as

God. A questioner often assumes that if Christians were only less bigoted they could change the rules of their club.

But entrance into the Kingdom of God is not determined, for example, as are the speed laws of a particular community. A ten-dollar fine for going through a stop sign is not inherent in the breaking of that law. A citizens' committee could easily get together and vote to reduce the fine to five dollars or raise it to fifty dollars.

But to break certain laws of the universe involves an inherent penalty. If you put your hand into a fire, you will get burned. A group of people could get together and pass a resolution that a person's hand would not be burned if he puts it into a fire, but this obviously would be futile. The result of breaking that law is inherent in the law itself.

Just as there are immutable physical laws in the universe, so there are immutable moral laws. An immutable law, inherent in the nature of Jesus Christ, makes it impossible to come to God in any other way than through Him, because *He is God.*

Dorothy Sayer's book, *The Mind of the Maker,* discusses this at some length.

Having said that Jesus Christ is the only way to God does not mean that other religions of the world are of no ethical and moral value. But this is not the same as bringing a person into vital relationship with the Living God. Man needs more than good advice. He needs power. His problem is not in knowing what he should do, but in failing to do it.

THE PROBLEM OF EVIL

A third frequent question is this: "If God is all good and all powerful, how can He allow babies to be born deformed or diseased? And how can He allow wars and suffering? Either He must be all good but not all powerful, or He must be all powerful but not all good."

Here again we must acknowledge that we do not have full knowledge of the origin of evil or the complete answer to the problem. But although many things are unknown to us, we do know some things. Evil came into the world as a result of man's deliberate rebellion against God. A man's actions are not limited to himself, but often involve other people. This is the way the universe is set up. God could stop war and stamp out evil, but if He began to judge every person righteously, who of us would stand till nightfall? Each of us must admit that he possesses the potential for incredible evil. Some of us have not gone the way of others because we have not yet been tempted in the same way.

God has done the greatest thing that He could possibly do to solve the problem of evil. He has given His Son, Jesus Christ, to die in our place in order that the problem of forgiveness can be solved personally. If we refuse His love and salvation, we have no one to blame but ourselves when we find ourselves personally still faced with the problem.

C. S. Lewis points out that it is useless to speculate about the origin of sin and evil. We are faced with the fact of evil and must come up with a solution to this. We must leave the academic problem, and address ourselves to the practical problem. H. Evans Hopkins in *The Mystery of Suffering* (Inter Varsity Press) and C. S. Lewis in *The Problem of Pain* discuss this in detail.

SCIENCE AND MIRACLES

Another frequent question involves the problem of miracles and the reality of the supernatural. Here it is important to get at the root premise of the question and not become bogged down in detail.

In other words, if someone asks you how it was possible for Jesus Christ to feed 5,000 people from five loaves and two fish, it is useless to discuss the details of that particular incident. Underlying the whole matter lies the question: "Does an all-powerful God exist?" If such a God exists, miracles are no problem intellectually. In fact, they might be expected. If God created the universe and the ordinary laws of the universe, He is capable of transcending them.

Once a Japanese friend of mine who was discussing Jesus

Christ said, "I find it impossible to believe that a man could become God." This helped me see his problem and I replied, "Neither could I believe that — but I can believe that God could become man." He saw it in a flash, and a week later became a Christian.

Various arguments give clues to the existence of God: the design in the universe indicates a designer; the existence of personalities suggests a Greater Personality (since no effect is greater than its cause); etc. But the greatest evidence that God exists is that He Himself lived on this planet in the person of Jesus Christ. The other ideas may give some hints, but can perhaps be refuted. The presence of Jesus Christ in history, however, removes all doubt, and confirms God's existence. Before a person can dismiss the idea of God, he must adequately explain Jesus Christ: who He is and what He did.

At this point it is important to see the fallacy of the frequent statement, "If you could prove God in a test tube for me, I would believe." This is nonsense, because it suggests that one approach, commonly called "the scientific method," is the only measure of reality. Actually many areas of reality cannot be measured or weighed. Who has ever seen a pound of justice or three feet of love, yet who would deny their reality?

Further, basic to the scientific method is the aspect of repeatability. History is inherently non-repeatable, and therefore outside the scope of the scientific method for verification. No one will ever repeat Napoleon. But because he cannot be submitted to the scientific method does not mean that he was not real.

There is, however, a science of history; and as we take its historical method and apply it to the life and death of Jesus Christ, we find an enormous amount of evidence to demonstrate His reality. Therefore, we must understand clearly the limitations of the test-tube type of scientific method and not be thrown off by this apparently telling question.

Science Is a Sacred Cow by Anthony Standen points out some common fallacies in such reasoning. *Miracles* by C. S. Lewis deals with this in some detail, as does Inter-Varsity's booklet, *Is Christianity Credible?* This material should be thought through by each Christian.

THE TRUSTWORTHINESS OF THE BIBLE

A fifth question relates to the reliability of the Scripture: "How do you reconcile faith with the fact that the Bible is full of errors?" or "Hasn't evolution shown that the Bible is unreliable?"

Since there is a great deal of vague thinking about errors in the Bible, it is good to ask the questioner what errors he has in mind. Often there are none and it is evident that he has not even read the Bible. (It would then be quite appropriate to suggest that he do so.)

The Christian should also master certain books that deal with the reliability of the Scriptures. *Are the New Testament Documents Reliable?* by F. F. Bruce (Inter-Varsity Press) contains some helpful chapters. Another good book for exhaustive reference is *Some Alleged Discrepancies in the Bible* by John Haley. This is a pretty complete reference book.

The question of evolution is a thorny one. However, since evolution is not the basic issue, it should not be discussed as though it were. Basically the problem is philosophical. Did God create the universe or didn't He? How He did it is secondary. Theories such as evolution can often be treated as descriptions and not explanations. It seems fairly well agreed that God created some basic kinds of life and that there has been wide variation within them.

(It is also important to point out that the Bible does not have any set chronology. The dates that appear in the margin of some editions are not part of the original text.)

The word evolution means different things to different people. If it is used to deny the reality of God as creator, and to suggest a complete naturalistic explanation of the universe, then its philosophical presupposition must be dealt with. Otherwise it is a secondary issue.

Remember that a person's salvation does not depend on his view of evolution but on whether he has ever personally received Jesus Christ. Jesus Christ should be made the issue.

The reliability of the New Testament from the historical point of view is more easily established. Modern archaeology has repeatedly confirmed Biblical history. Books by William M. Ramsay and Frederic Kenyon give some evidence, as well as the one by F. F. Bruce mentioned above. Recently a leading Jewish archaeologist, Dr. Nelson Glueck said, "It can be categorically stated that no archaeological discovery has ever controverted a Biblical reference" (*Rivers in the Desert*, Jewish Publishing Society, p. 31).

Helpful books on the general subject of the inspiration of the Scripture are *Fundamentalism and the Word of God* by J. I. Packer (available from Inter-Varsity) and *The Christian View of Science and Scripture* by Bernard Ramm (Eerdmans Publishing Co., Grand Rapids). See also *Revelation and the Bible*, edited by Carl F. H. Henry (Baker Book House, Grand Rapids).

I'M GOOD ENOUGH

The final question is this: "Isn't a good life sufficient to enable a person to enter heaven? If a man has lived a good moral life and done the best he can to qualify for the presence of God, why must he receive Jesus Christ?"

Such a question displays a low view of the holiness of God and a high, unrealistic view of the moral goodness of man. God's holiness is infinite, while no man has ever been perfect in his actions, let alone in his thoughts and motivations.

As an illustration of the necessity of receiving Jesus Christ, I often use the possibility of swimming to Hawaii. Let us think of Hawaii as God's absolute standard of holiness which we must reach in our own strength if on the basis of our lives, we are to come into the presence of God.

Suppose now that every person who ever lived were lined up on the shore of California. Let's say that those who have lived a very good moral life could swim fifty miles out into the ocean; those who have lived an average life, three or four miles out; and those who are moral derelicts merely flounder in the surf a hundred yards off shore.

Comparing man with man, the difference between the morally upright man who is able to swim fifty miles, and the derelict in the surf is enormous. But with reference to the goal of swimming to Hawaii, both have one thing in common. Neither comes near Hawaii.

So it is in the moral realm. Individuals differ greatly in terms of their own moral life. But with reference to God's absolute holy standard they are on the same footing. Each one must be taken by Jesus Christ and His righteousness to the goal of God's perfection if he is going to enter into the presence of God.

These are just a few of the questions that most frequently arise in the minds of non-Christians. Once a person has thought them through in his own mind, it is not so likely that he will be caught off guard by non-Christians' questions.

And when a question comes up which he cannot answer, the Christian should begin to look for an answer. He shouldn't be discouraged even if the first ten people he asks don't have the answer. The fact that he and his immediate friends don't have it doesn't mean that no answer is possible. Nor is it primarily a matter of intellectual ability or inability, since brilliant men who are Christians are in most fields of study.

Remember too that a non-Christian's failure to accept an answer doesn't necessarily render that answer invalid. A person who is unwilling to believe won't accept anything as evidence. Many intelligent people don't believe for the same reason that many unintelligent people don't believe: they are unwilling to accept the inevitable change that Jesus Christ will require in their lives.

Yet if God begins to soften hearts, answers to these questions can be of immense help.*

*HIS Magazine (November, 1960) pp. 1-4. This article is available in reprint form from HIS Reprints, 4605 Sherwood, Downers Grove, Illinois 60515, prepaid only, 25 for $2.00 or 100 for $7.00. Reprinted by permission from HIS, student magazine of Inter-Varsity Christian Fellowship © 1960.

If you have found this paper helpful I would refer you to Paul Little's other two books, in which he has more detailed statements concerning these questions. In *How to Give Away Your Faith,* one chapter is devoted to this subject, while in *Know Why You Believe* twelve key questions are investigated.

I. INTRODUCTION

    1. Douglas Hyde, *Dedication and Leadership: Learning from the Communists* (Notre Dame, Indiana: Notre Dame Press, and London: Sands & Co., 1966), pp. 25-26.

II. CHAPTER ONE: *The Principles of Witness*

    1. Leighton Ford, *The Christian Persuader* (London: Hodder and Stoughton, and New York: Harper and Row, 1966), p. 46.

    2. Mark 16:15 (Phillips Translation).

    3. H. Wakelin Coxill and Sir Kenneth Grubb (eds.), *World Christian Handbook* (London: Lutterworth Press, 1967).

    4. Ford, pp. 48-50. This is not, however, to deny the gift of evangelism which God gives to certain men. It is evident that some people are especially effective in the communication of the Gospel to others. One need only look at the book of Acts to see this. Peter and Paul had this gift. It is, however, to say that this gift of evangelism is not meant to be exercised in isolation. The error we have fallen into is that of thinking that the evangelist must do the whole job of evangelism — and hence abdicating our responsibility as laymen. The gift of evangelism given certain men is exercised to its greatest extent when it is used within the context of a witnessing church.

    5. The other problem, of course, is that not everyone who hears the Gospel will respond positively. But this is not our concern. The Great Commission states that our task is simply to *present* the Gospel, not to ensure results.

    6. H. R. Weber, "The Spontaneous Missionary Church," *Laity,* Volume IV (May, 1962), p. 75. Note that this article is included in Chapter One in an adapted form, as the Supplementary Reading.

    7. *Ibid.,* p. 72.

    8. *Ibid.,* p. 73.

    9. Named after Kenneth Strachan, the former director of the Latin America Mission who did much of this research.

    10. *Evangelism-in-Depth: Experimenting with a New Type of Evangelism* (Chicago: Moody Press, 1961), p. 25.

All the information concerning Latin America Mission is taken from this book.

11. Leighton Ford, *Letters to a New Christian* (Minneapolis and London: The Billy Graham Evangelistic Association, 1967), p. 43.
12. I Peter 3:15 (Phillips Translation).
13. Ford, pp. 43-44.

III. CHAPTER TWO: *The Problems of Witness*

1. See John White's paper reprinted in chapter 3 for an excellent illustration of what happened when some Bible school students dared to admit that they did not know certain answers about Christianity.
2. John Carter; *Methods of Mission in Southern Africa* (London: S.P.C.K., 1963), p. 99.
3. John White, "Witnessing is not Brainwashing," *HIS,* XXVI (June, 1966), p. 6. Note that this article is reprinted as the supplementary reading for Chapter 3.
4. James 2:15-16 (Phillips Translation).
5. Mark 1:15. (All scripture references are from the R.S.V. unless otherwise noted).
6. White, p. 5.

IV. CHAPTER THREE: *The Practice of Witness*

1. This exercise is taken from: A. J. T. Cook, *Handbook of Lay Involvement* (Johannesburg; unpublished; copied by the author), p. 26.
2. Paul Tournier, in his introduction to *Setting Men Free* by Bruce Larson (Grand Rapids, Michigan: Zondervan Publishing House, 1967), p. 8.
3. White, pp. 5 and 6 (italics mine).
4. Larson, *Setting Men Free,* pp. 27 and 28.
5. Hyde, pp. 97 and 98.
6. Samuel Shoemaker, *The Experiment of Faith* (New York: Harper and Row, 1957), pp. 13-14.
7. Note in Mark 2:14-17, that Matthew (called here Levi) begins his discipleship with Jesus by inviting his friends and colleagues into his home to meet Jesus. Throughout the New Testament, homes are used constantly for worship, prayer, counselling, evangelism, etc.
8. Shoemaker, p. 14.
9. Paul Tournier, *Escape From Loneliness* (Philadelphia: The Westminster Press, and London: S.C.M. Press, 1962), p. 13.

10. Weber, p. 74-75 (italics mine).
11. William Barclay, *The Gospel of Mark* ("The Daily Study Bible"; Edinburgh: The Saint Andrew Press, 1957), p. 116.

V. CHAPTER FOUR: *Preparation for Witness*

1. John 17.
2. Matthew 5:13.
3. Ford, *The Christian Persuader,* pp. 71 and 72.
4. However, let me reiterate once again: "Let your love be genuine" (Romans 12:9). Your motivation cannot be to seek friendship *in order to witness.* You love others because this is what Christianity is all about. Of course, part of love is openness about Christ.
5. Rosalind Rinker, *Prayer: Conversing with God* (Grand Rapids: Zondervan Publishing House, 1959), pp. 68-72.
6. It is interesting to note in Matthew 7:1 ("Judge not, that you be not judged") that judgment has a built-in penalty. When we judge others, their inevitable response is to judge us in return — and this hurts. If you doubt this principle, observe what happens the next time you judge someone!
7. For example, there are the L.P. records, "Another Week to Go," recorded by "Jonathan and Charles" (pop music); and "There's More to Living Than I Know so Far," recorded by Linda Rich (folk-music); both issued by Inter-Varsity Records (Downers Grove, Illinois, U.S.A.). Avant Garde Records have also issued a series of records of modern Christian music of various types. In *Background to the Task* (Scripture Union, 1968) there is an interesting article by Colin Chapman entitled "Modern Music and Evangelism."
8. See the Group Leader's Manual for the outline of such an evening.
9. John 15:4-6, 7.

VI. CHAPTER FIVE: *The Small Group and Witness*

1. For a detailed study of conversational prayer, see Rinker, *Prayer: Conversing With God.*
2. Rinker, p. 82.
3. Bruce Larson, *Dare to Live Now!* (Grand Rapids: Zondervan Publishing House, 1965), p. 87.
4. George and Florence Pert, *Get Going Through Small*

Groups (Carmel, New York: Guideposts Associates, Inc., 1969), p. 19.

5. Clyde Reid, *Groups Alive — Church Alive* (New York: Harper & Row, 1969), p. 47.

6. *Ibid.,* p. 48.

7. A word of caution is necessary at this point. A group must not be tempted to try to become a "therapy group" unless there is professional leadership. In an actual therapy group there is a deliberate attempt to bring hidden feelings and fears to the surface so people can learn to cope with them. This is something which can only be done successfully by an expert. Great harm can result if a group deliberately releases these inner forces and yet does not know how to cope with them.

8. Dietrich Bonhoeffer, *Life Together* (London: S.C.M. Press, and New York: Harper and Row, 1949), p. 86.

9. D. T. Niles, *That They May Have Life* (New York: Harper and Row, 1961), p. 96.

10. Samuel Shoemaker, quoted in Pert, p. 17.

11. Bruce Larson, "A New Breed of Men," *Groups in Action,* ed. Lyman Coleman (Newtown, Pennsylvania: The Halfway House, 1968), p. 56.

12. I am not suggesting, however, that one walk into a group and "hang up all one's dirty linen in public." Such behavior, at times, is exhibitionism, not honesty. The nature of the group will define the bounds of sharing. The key thing though is *no pretense.*

13. Paul Miller, *Group Dynamics in Evangelism* (Scottdale, Pennsylvania: Herald Press, 1958), p. 93.

VII. CHAPTER SIX: *The Content of Witness (Part 1)*

1. Ford, *The Christian Persuader,* p. 93.

2. Romans 8:28.

3. Hyde, pp. 115-116.

4. For a Biblical statement of this principle see James 1, especially as it is rendered in J. B. Phillips' version.

5. Ephesians 6:12.

6. C. S. Lewis, *Christian Reflections* (Grand Rapids: Wm. B. Eerdmans Publishing Co., and London: Geoffrey Bles, Ltd., 1967), p. 33, used by permission.

7. Acts 2:36.

8. A word is in order about witness by means of sharing our "testimony," i.e. our experience of conversion. This is well and good; and of great value, especially since thereby people come to realize that God does still change

lives. Yet we cannot stop there. Such witness centers on *our experience of Christ.* We must move on from this point to *Christ Himself.*

However, sharing our experience of Christ is a normal part of witness. This is why you were asked in the Bible study in Chapter 3 to write out what Jesus has done for you. In Chapter 7, you will be given further opportunity to think about your own experience of Christianity. Personal experience often forms the *initial* aspect of sharing.

One more comment about testimonies. They can become stereotyped, i.e. they can sound like a speech which we have memorized and repeat mechanically. When this happens they lose that ring of freshness which is their great value.

9. C. S. Lewis, "What are We to Make of Jesus Christ?" *Asking them Questions,* quoted in Clyde S. Kilby (ed.), *A Mind Awake* (London: Geoffrey Bles, and New York: Harper and Row, 1968), p. 92.

10. C. S. Lewis, *Mere Christianity* (London: Geoffrey Bles, and New York: Harper & Row, 1952), pp. 52-53.

11. I Peter 3:18.

12. Lewis, pp. 54-55.

13. Revelation 3:20.

14. John 1:12.

VIII. CHAPTER SEVEN: *The Content of Witness (Part 2)*

1. This exercise was suggested to me in Coleman, *Groups in Action,* Agenda No. 1.

2. Shoemaker, *The Experiment of Faith,* p. 45.

3. It is well to note that what I am suggesting is not the reshaping of the gospel message itself. We have no right or authority to do this. In fact, such an endeavor would be worse than futile; it would be criminal, because we would not just be pawning off on people some of our own ideas that have no inherent power or truth, but in fact we would be *preventing* individuals from coming in contact with the actual life-changing Gospel. However, while we must take care not to tamper with the *essence* of the Gospel, we must at the same time feel free to change the forms through which this message is expressed, if by so doing we enable outsiders really to understand this Gospel. For example, the concept of sin is central to the Gospel message. We dare not say, for the sake of com-

munication, "Man is not sinful. He is basically good."
Apart from being untrue, this would undercut the whole
meaning of the atonement. To do this would be to tamper with the essence of our message. But on the other
hand, "Sin is a word that does not communicate in our
society today. People usually think of *My Sin* perfume
by Lanvin or immorality of one kind or another. If they
don't happen to be guilty of this kind of immorality,
they become highly incensed because they do not see
themselves as sinners in these terms." (Little, p. 57).
Yet virtually everyone today is aware, in one way or another, that something is radically wrong with the world
and with himself. This is an awareness of sin, even
though it is not labled with that word. To communicate
the concept of sin (which we must) we must therefore
discuss it in terms by which men in fact experience it,
e.g. loneliness, lack of purpose, guilt, etc.

4. Burton Harding, "The Content of the Gospel," *HIS* Magazine (Reprints of articles, January to October, 1966),
   p. 5.
5. *Ibid.*
6. Mary McDermott Shideler, *A Creed for a Christian
   Skeptic* (Grand Rapids: Wm. B. Eerdmans Publishing
   Co., 1968), p. 95. Used by permission.
7. *Ibid.*, p. 98.
8. Ephesians 2:1-5 (J. B. Phillips).
9. Shideler, pp. 36-37.
10. Paul Little, *How to Give Away Your Faith* (Chicago:
    Inter-Varsity Press, 1966), p. 59.
11. Shideler, p. 100.
12. Romans 3:23.
13. Matthew 7:1.
14. John R. W. Stott, *Basic Christianity* (London: Inter-Var-
    sity Fellowship, and Grand Rapids: Wm. B. Eerdmans
    Publishing Co., 1958), p. 131.

You may well ask how such an act of commitment relates to infant baptism and confirmation. In baptism,
vows are made on behalf of the infant by the parents.
Furthermore, the parents vow to raise the child in the
Christian faith, so that at confirmation a child is ready
to take upon himself these vows made for him. He
"confirms" that as an adult he does want to follow Christ.

But again, the emphasis cannot be placed only on the
subjective side. As in conversion, so also in baptism and
confirmation, what God is doing is even more important
than what we are doing. It is God's action, not our re-

sponse to it, or apprehension of it that is of primary and ultimate importance.

15. Little, pp. 56 and 57.
16. In memorizing verses it is often helpful to put them on cards, and carry these cards with you. You can then memorize and review in the odd spare moments you have during the day.

IX. CHAPTER EIGHT: *The Strategy of Witness*

1. Ford, p. 89.
2. See the sketch of a suggested plan of evangelism in the Introduction.
3. See the supplementary reading in chapter one.
4. I Peter 2:9 (italics mine).
5. Hyde, p. 93.
6. Colossians 1:16 and 2:15.
7. John 15:16.

NOTES

NOTES

NOTES

NOTES

41837